I would like to dedicate this book to all those poor lost souls who committed the ultmate act of suicide, whilst not having the will nor the means to fight their own fight. I could have been one of them!

May God go with you.

Contents

Chapter 1

FINDING MY FEET

I liked being a mechanic. It was the hands- on work that appealed to me first day. I loved the feel of tools and working with metal. I was always a closet racer; I wanted to be a rally driver but figured the best way in was by learning about cars firstly. I was driving since I was 12 years old. I used to take my fathers car for drives in the countryside in the early mornings. It was exhilarating, freedom behind the wheel. Working with cars was great therapy, it was very satisfying. The ulterior motive with me was always to go for a burn, once the job was done.

I went to st Brendan's college in Killarney, where football was king, and if you were into any other sport, you were an outsider. I got a good education there, but it wasn't my favourite place in the world. I was never the academic type, never wanted to be, though I tried. I tried to be lots of different things, mainly to appease others, but I was a rebel without a cause, I always felt out of place in st Brendan's. I had bundles of energy, could run and run and run until I dropped. In hindsight, I should have been an athlete, as I had ferocious drive and competitive spirit. I still have today, but it is tempered with the knowledge that I have to look after myself physically and mentally.

St Brendan's could be a brutal school at times, discipline was dished out with random acts of violence perpetuated by so called disciples of Jesus, some of whom took out their life's frustrations with devastating impact on the few who happened to be in their bad books. I witnessed first hand such acts of violence, with the aggressor becoming more and more wound up as the level of violence increased, it was like they took pleasure in administering pain.

In hindsight, I should have been sent to Killarney Technical School, where you could study different hands- on trades like metal work, welding, pipe fitting and so on. I always loved tinkling with bikes as a lad; I would take them apart and rebuild them on a regular basis. I spent so many days going to Billy Ahearn's cycle shop in high street looking for bits and bobs and getting wheels straightened after many an epic out in the national park. Billy always fixed me up; he was a great man with a sense of humour to match.

Mechanics are a strange breed. They have to balance so many things at once, how best to please the customer, how to enhance your reputation, how to price the job so the customer returns loyally again and again. You have to weigh up the likelihood of a part lasting 5,000 more kms, or failing in 1000 k. Make the wrong call and you'll lose the customer and possibly do extensive damage to an engine or transmission. Save them a couple of hundred quid and you're a hero until your next job. It is like a production line of sorts. You never repeat identical jobs, as the work is varied and interesting, not to mention physically demanding. Mechanics are a tough bunch. Pride and ego are very high in their world.

I went to San Francisco in '78, to work for a cousin. He had a garage in San Mateo, South of the city. I took a Freddie Laker flight from Gatwick at the time, and it was a great adventure, a whole new exciting world. I flew to Heathrow first and then transferred by helicopter to Gatwick, along with a handful of business types who were very smartly dressed in pin striped suits, whereas I was dressed in Levi jeans and a lovely down jacket I bought in Piccadilly Circus. It was my first time in a helicopter and I loved every minute of the trip.

I landed in LA and spent a night in the Vista Motel, a dodgy looking joint if I ever saw one. The smog was horrible, in fact choking. The following day I made my way to San Francisco and to my cousin's garage. I arrived at his premises one beautiful sunny morning and was met seemingly reluctantly by John. He was a little apprehensive about the prospect of looking after me and I was a little uneasy settling in to the alien routine.

On the car lot sat a number of Jaguars alongside many American made cars. I think he wanted to push the European cars rather than the American models as there was a much better profit margin in those exotic Jaguars. I wasn't happy about his methods as he went to extraordinary lengths in order to rebuild old parts that would have long been discarded back home. I suppose every buck counted and he had a family to feed as well.

Working in the lovely warm sunny weather was a tonic; even my spanners were hot to the touch if I left them out in the heat for too long. That was in complete contrast to working back home, where the incessant rain and cold made working conditions terrible, particularly so when a car came in after a particularly wet morning, you would be like a wet rag on occasions, not funny.

I was quickly getting accustomed to the American way, as at lunch time John went out and bought a few bottles of Bud. I didn't really want to drink that early in the day, but the novelty of doing so inspired me to go with the trend, but only for a short while. I always wanted to be alert and working under my own influence rather than any outside influences.

I went to a car auction and I ended up with a lovely Mazda rx4, rotary powered. I loved the sound of it; it was really different from the 4 strokes. One weekend night, I wanted to drive into the city and my cousin gave me his phone number, just in case I got lost, and a map. I was very eager to see the city and on the way in I saw the flashing blue lights of a police car in my mirror, and I pulled over. The police officer said I could spend the night in jail if the officer so wished. However, he left me off with a stern warning, after I told him I was on holidays and would be going back home the following week. Of course I was speeding, I was in a hurry.

I visited a few bars and a Chinese restaurant, where my mouth almost combusted after the very hot spicy meal. As I made my way home I couldn't get on to the freeway, and I must have gone over that Golden Gate bridge at least twice, I was heading North instead of South. I gave up and booked into a downtown hotel for the night, and when I got home the following morning, my cousin berated me for not phoning him. I had lost the telephone number.

There was a stewards inquiry at the house in the early morning, John said that he hadn't slept the night with worry and thought I was mugged or in a hospital somewhere. I was taken aback with his reaction and I tried to allay his fears by saying I could look after myself, he needn't have worried so much.

I loved the laid back attitude of the West Coast, the beautiful beaches, the pacific highway along route 1, the beautiful drive along the Coast. I loved watching the surfers ride the surf, the balmy sunsets. I went to LA one weekend to see a NASCAR race, and it was really different, all that rolling thunder. Glen Campbell, the Rhinestone Cowboy himself was singing the Stars and Stripes before the race got underway. The grandstands were full to capacity with people swigging beer and munching big fat burgers, the American way. Everybody seemed to be obsessed with making a buck, any which way you could. I shared a camper van with a work mate on this journey to LA and it was nice to drive down there for a weekend, as I was getting cabin fever in the house I was staying in, as I was a guest there and had no real freedom.

I was walking around San Francisco one morning when I was approached by this nice woman; well she seemed interested in me anyhow. What I didn't realise was that she was recruiting people for the church of the Latter Day Saints. She invited me up to her office for a coffee and a chat and it was from that point on that the mind games began. I was a terribly gullible lad and easily influenced, and she succeeded in out psyching me and tried to convince me that wealth and materialism were not the holy grail of life. She wanted to indoctrinate me into becoming a Mormon, and I went along with it, I even gave her my cousin's phone number so she could contact me.

My cousin was very anxious to know who this woman was when the phone rang, and eventually I told him the story. He was shell shocked and told me that these people were brainwashing individuals in order to subscribe to their church. I took no notice and carried on with the meetings for a while. I was hardly in California for a wet week at that stage.

Eventually, after a few consultations, I was called in to the office to be interviewed by a church elder. He was trying to determine what business I was in back home. Here was I, a fresh faced innocent boy, just off the plane on my first transatlantic foray, and this guy figured me to be a business man of some sort. He wanted to know whether I had any money. I told him a big fib, that I had a garage full of old jaguars back home and that I was restoring them to concours condition and then selling them off to the rich and famous. He sat up instantly, very interested in my business all of a sudden. It was then that I twigged what was happening, and I took off in a cloud of rubber smoke, despite arranging another appointment with him for the following week. I wasn't that gullible after all. So much for idealism!

John was very anxious to stop any further contact with these Mormon people, but he need not have worried, I figured it out for myself.

In the early eighties I moved to London, having been stifled by constraints at home, and being imprisoned in a workshop environment. I had itchy feet, the world was waiting for me, and I was ready. I suppose I was very naive about the ways of the world, I was totally innocent. I believed that if you worked hard, then everything else would follow, automatically.

I got a job with British Leyland in their Park Royal depot, where they stored and prepared their cars before sending them on to the dealers. I was employed as a driver. I loved driving the brand new jaguars, especially the v 12 5.3 litre XJ 12. There was a strip of concrete road for about 200 metres on the drive to the storage area, and it was out of sight of the main building. I used to stop the car and let it warm up for a few minutes, then floor the throttle to the max and do a nought to sixty count in the little space available. I loved the cloud of tyre smoke that engulfed the car in the aftermath. I could have been heard miles away but I didn't care, I was pumped up. Thereafter, I would mosey along down to park the car nicely in the car park. One careful owner and the car covered only 500 metres.

I often thought about the people who would eventually drive these cars, sober stiff upper lipped types, chauffeurs to multi national companies, rock stars of the ages, drug runners and inner city London criminals, using the cars for ferrying their illegal bounty around the city. I wondered did they get the same kick out of driving them as I had. I didn't need drugs to get me off, this was my drug, and I was in ecstasy.

Cars were supplied and prepared for Royalty duties here also, lovely big black limousines, Rolls Royce's, Bentleys, Jaguars, not to mention the numerous Land Rovers and Range Rovers, used in their sumptuous country estates. The lovely smell from the leather hide upholstery was like perfume to me. Left hand drive limousines and jeeps were regularly shipped to Africa, which astounded me somewhat. I loved driving the left hand drive cars, it had an exotic feeling. I was instantly transported to all these countries where one drove on the right side of the road.

Whilst a student in the presentation monastery in primary school, we were regularly asked to give a penny to the "Black Babies" in Africa, whilst not having a clue as to the recipient of all of those pennies, but in our wildest imagination, we could have never foreseen the money being used for such decadent purposes, images of lines of Jaguars parading in perfect symmetry in the various ostentatious displays by the numerous African dictators in the midst of terrible poverty and subjugation of their own people. I was with them in heart.

I loved motor sport of all types, especially rallying, and in particular, the World Rally Championship in the late seventies – early eighties. I wanted to be one of those drivers, I knew I had the talent, but there wasn't a hope in hell that I could even afford a standard car, things were very depressed in those days. Rally drivers were treated like rock stars everywhere they went. My bible at that time was Motoring News and Auto sport magazine.

I couldn't wait for Thursday mornings to come, when both magazines were published. I devoured every article within, scrutinised every detail of the reports on whatever world championship rally was in progress. I knew every driver by name and his driving history, what team he drove for, how a new development car was being tested down in Boreham, Fords official test track in Surrey. It was an army testing ground used for military vehicles. Ford would bring their ford escorts there in the seventies and early eighties and drive the cars until destruction, in preparation for rallies like the African Safari. I thought of little else, everything I did revolved around getting to a rally somewhere, or being stuck under the bonnet of a car.

At one stage in London, I applied for a job in a bank, mainly under pressure from home, to get a secure job with a pension and all the perks. This was the "Holy Grail" back home; get a nice cushy number in the bank and just go with the flow, you were there! I worked for three months for Allied Irish Finance in Wembley and I can honestly say that I hated every minute there. Firstly, I had to wear a suit and tie, which I hadn't done since my first communion. I felt like a monkey in a cage. As far as I could gather, most of the other employees were unhappy there. For the first two weeks, I was writing up expenses for various reps in the UK. I was very popular as I kept getting phone calls from the reps to make sure their monthly expenses were sent out. I had a lot of friends on the road, and I liked that bit of contact.

Eventually, after three months I couldn't take it any longer. I was called to the manager's office and asked why I was not wearing a shirt and tie. That was akin to having a rope around my neck, and I wasn't going to conform, so I left the job. The lure of mechanics was too strong, the hands on passion I had for the job was impossible to ignore.

I loved going to Speakers Corner in Hyde Park, where anyone could rant and rave or pontificate on any subject under the sun, absolutely no constraints, it was pure entertainment. Just bring your soap box and rant away. I envied those speakers, their brashness, their astonishing witticisms, their challenging unconventional thinking.

I scouted around job centres in London and I got a start in this rough looking garage in Harlesden, not a particularly glamorous place, lots of African immigrants and West Indian characters whom I got on great with. The reason I wanted to work there was because I had a look at the cars in the garage, and they were mainly Porsche and BMW's as well as the bread and butter stuff. I wanted to get experience on those particular cars, but I was thrown in at the murky end and ended up on my back replacing clutches for the first few weeks.

There was no such thing as a ramp or even a pit, the essential bottom drawer tool for any mechanic. I need not have gone to any gym as I spent most of the day lowering gearboxes onto my chest and lining up the clutch with my eyes in order to mate up the gearbox to the clutch. If you were a wee bit out of alignment, you would get away with it, but anymore and you would end up bench pressing a gearbox for up to half an hour, sweat rolling down your face and chest. But once it mated up, everything was tickety boo and I could take forty winks on my back, occasionally rattling a spanner to make it seem like I was still working.

There were a lot of dodgy practices going on here. A fellow employee, an Irish lad from Mayo, was doing most of the Porsche and BMW work, and I would help him when he was ready to install the engine and gearbox after a rebuild. I loved that as we got on great, he was a hard grafter and I learned a lot from him. Only later on, I realised what was happening, when it came to invoicing customers.

A full engine rebuild on a Porsche flat 6 engine was costing around 3000 quid, ferocious money in those days, but only a cosmetic job was done to the engine. The piston rings were replaced, the cylinder bores were honed and the valve seats refaced with the original valves, yet they were charging for all new items. Sometimes an engine was just given a steam clean and the customer was charged for replacing the head gasket, it was totally corrupt. There was something else going on also which I couldn't quiet understand, but was very dubious, may have involved drugs. I was just a naive young lad trying to make my way up the ladder, none of my business.

I could not continue working here, as conditions were dreadful, and I didn't want to be part of a rip-off operation, conning poor people of their hard earned cash. This was 1980, and times were tough in London as well as Ireland.

London in those days was a hive of activity, what with all the freshly qualified Irish people coming out of College, lots of them making their way down to Murphy Construction. Joseph Murphy, a Caherciveen native, founded the company in the late fifties- early sixties from his own sweat and blood, and went on to become an iconic name in London for years to come. He was a God to those guys, most of whom never put a hand to a shovel in their lives. Any major construction site in the city was surrounded by huge advertising hoardings with the name of "MURPHY" in huge letters all over them.

Kilburn and Cricklewood were the pick up points in the early hours, if you wanted a labouring job. It was a bit like prostitution, you lined up for work with all and sundry, but the fittest and strongest looking got priority. As the years rolled on, jobs became scarcer and with the influx of Eastern Europeans, it got more competitive. Paddy was threatened, as he was no longer top dog in the line, and he was aging also, his lifestyle was catching up with him, unable to match the fit and tough youngsters coming down the line. I didn't want to go down that road.

I went back to the job centre and saw an advertisement that appealed to me. It was with the Saab importer in Acton Town, a five star workshop, heated, with regular breaks and an incentive scheme. It was early December 1980 when I started working there, and Christmas was in the door. I had only worked there for three weeks when I was invited to stay the night in a lovely hotel in the West End for their annual Christmas party, and boy was I chuffed. Everything was free, I was in heaven, great Cockneys and a few Afro-Caribbean's thrown in, dancing all night to reggae music. It was an eclectic mix and worked brilliantly, I couldn't believe my luck.

The workshop was a hive of activity, very industrious. A few of the Cockneys approached me and told me I was showing them up, as my work rate was way above theirs. I was told to slow down the pace. If a car had to have a quick turn around service, I would have it done in half the allowed time, thus I was very popular with the service manager; he too was Afro Caribbean, a lovely man. We shared an interest in Motor Sport and got on very well. We had a competition to see who could change the Turbocharger the fastest in a Saab 900, and I won, I did it in fifteen minutes flat, starting with a red hot engine, ample buckets of water being used to cool down the turbo firstly.

After a service, I would drive the cars around a route that passed Wormwood Scrubs prison, and it was a challenging route with lovely sweeping corners. One of the tests we did was to check the boost pressure on the turbocharged engines, which involved connecting a boost gauge to the inlet manifold and routing it into the dashboard, then driving the car and whist braking with the left foot and at the same time accelerating enough to get the engine fully stressed and taking a reading. It was akin to a formula one qualifying lap to me, the smell of burning brake pads, the popping of the waste gate on the turbo, the strain on the engine which seemed about to detonate at any second, especially if the boost pressure was too high. It was invigorating, I was a natural for this kind of work, and I loved it.

The lure of getting involved in motorsport was too strong and I would scour Auto Sport magazine every Thursday, looking to find a way into motorsport in any capacity. Whilst in Acton Town, I came across an alladins cave workshop. It was David Sutton Motorsport, a renowned Ford Escort preparation expert who ran privateer drivers in ex- works cars. These were cars built by the ford factory for professionally contracted drivers. They would normally rally these cars for a year and then sell them off at the end of the season. David Sutton would be the main beneficiary, as he was noted to be one of the finest car preparation experts at the time.

I walked into this workshop one day out of curiosity, and I was smitten. There were six Ford Escorts in various stages of build on the floor, along with various engines awaiting their home. Magical names like the infamous BDA engine, which every rally follower in the world would know about, also a BDG engine on the ground, which was a development engine to be used for tarmac cars. Of course I was instantly attracted to all the exotic rally locations around the world as well as the cars.

I didn't want to leave; I wanted to sleep on the floor with all that adrenaline around me. I spoke to a couple of mechanics and they told me there were no jobs going as he ran a very tight outfit, on a fraction of the budget of the works teams. But I persisted and wrote a letter to David Sutton himself asking for a job. I was called to interview and boy, was I excited. I went down to the workshop and found him to be a perfect gentleman, but ultimately he had no vacancy, money was tight, even though I'd have worked for nothing, except there were the mundane living expenses one had to survive on.

In the corner of the workshop stood a lovely black ford escort, nicknamed "Black Beauty" and later driven by Ari Vatanen in a few rounds of the Irish tarmac championship in the eighties. It was magic seeing that car just freshly built with a lovely fresh paint job.

I was disappointed at not getting the job, but I still applied to anything that involved Motorsport, and eventually my persistence paid off. I was living in a hostel in Notting Hill at this time, and whilst it was comfortable, I found it stifling, as I missed the open spaces of the country and that freedom to be able to get on a bike or run a mountain and jump in a lake all in the one afternoon. This place was too regimental for me.

The final straw with me came when I had to share a room with this nerd, who would get up at 2am and start washing his clothes in the small room, to my consternation. My mail was also opened before I received it, so that was the final straw for me. I didn't know whether it was the same geek, but I was out of there.

Most weekends were spent in Brands Hatch, watching motor sport and also taking in motor cycle meets. I would get the bus from London and it was great getting out in the countryside. On a couple of occasions, I travelled up to Yorkshire to see the RAC World Championship Rally. It was awesome to see those drivers racing through the forestry tracks, despite the murky weather.

I applied for a job with a racing car manufacturer in Norfolk, East Anglia. The company was called "Argo"; they built and supplied Formula Three single seater racing cars, mainly to privateers. I got a start there in January 1981, so it was with great disappointment that I announced the news to the lovely Saab people in London. They were sorry to see me go, and I too was a little nervous about leaving them, but I had no regrets, it was onwards and upwards for me.

I moved up to a small village called Thetford, and the factory was only a fifteen minute drive To Griston, another tiny hamlet with just one shop and plenty of old English charm. I loved the morning drive to work as you would drive down a narrow road between fields of glistening gold barley on either side of the road.

On my first morning I was introduced to various staff members and shown the workshop and drawing room, where the designer squirreled away, wracking his brain trying to find the perfect mix between performance, aerodynamics, weight, engine and transmission variables, plus all the other dynamics involved. It was intriguing for me, coming from a very basic background of run of the mill donkey work, to this fascinating environment where everything was designed and manufactured in-house, apart from the engine and transmission. It was challenging to say the least. I was in heaven.

I was introduced to Tony Di Gennaro, the number one mechanic and car builder whom I would be working under. Tony was a lovely fellow, and we instantly had a great rapport. Being Italian, he had much in common with me as I think the Irish and Italians are complementary to each other. He was a fastidious worker, meticulous in every detail. We would be assembling a Formula Three car from scratch; from the drawings in the designer's office, to the monocoque fabricated just a few metres away from us, to the welder and fabricator who made all the suspension components, then to the painter for a final coating of the glass fibre. I loved the work, it was very challenging, and nothing was left to chance.

Tony told me that they had a fantastic season the previous year, won a number of races and finished in the top three of the Formula Three Championship. That car was very tried and tested, but this new car was a totally different design. The previous year's car was of a space frame design, which basically means it was made from tubular metal and the new car was more in line with aircraft construction techniques. It was going to be an aluminium monocoque, with the engine and gearbox bolted onto the back of what we called "The Tub". The idea was to have much better structural rigidity, less flexing of the chassis, less body roll and more speed, hopefully. Orders were placed for twenty cars by mid January, but not one was completed at this stage. The orders came as a result of the previous year's performance, as it was deemed to be the car to beat.

I would go home in the evening after work, and after dinner, I would hear the door bell. It was Nick, the factory manager, asking if I could come to work that night to finish a car. I didn't hesitate, and worked all night, got home at 7 am and was back to work by 9 am. There was no extra pay for this but I liked it, it was a good learning experience. I didn't realise that this was going to be the norm, but I stuck with it for the time being.

I loved the industrious atmosphere, the adrenaline it produced, the opportunity of being involved with a professional race team and driver. If you wanted to drive one of these cars for the season, firstly you would have gained a reputation in Formula Ford racing. This was how many racing drivers came to notoriety and fame; thenceforth they would be spotted by team managers from the various constructors and would be offered works drives, as long as they brought sponsors money with them. Some of these drivers originated from South America and further afield, and they would usually have loads of money to do a seasons racing. They would bring a team with them, and once they paid the bounty upfront, they would bring their mechanics to the factory and build their own cars, under supervision from experienced factory personnel.

The engines were generally Toyota Nova Motors, which were supplied by an Italian firm. A driver would arrive at the factory with engines on a regular basis, but they all had to be paid for on delivery, no haggling. There was also an engine builder in the factory who was a Kiwi by the name of Don. After 500 racing miles, he would strip the engines and replace all rod bolts, head bolts and so on, and rebalance the pistons, replace bearings and any suspect parts. He worked in a tiny room, no bigger than your average utility room off any kitchen. He was determined to keep the room dust free, as any impurities in the air would contaminate his work in progress.

My favourite engine at the time was the Formula Atlantic BDD engine; it was a variant of the infamous BDA engine, which dominated rallying in the seventies and eighties. I loved the sound of those engines at full throttle; it was sensory stimulation on a huge scale. They had a very specific sound, and you knew for miles before a car appeared that it was powered by a BDA engine, it was that distinctive.

It was late January by the time the first car was completed, and it was taken to Snetterton Racetrack for a run to see how it performed. As the weather was sub zero and the track was damp, no useful information was gained from this test, bar running a basic systems check. After a couple of more frustrating runs it was decided that the car would be taken to a track in Italy, where weather conditions invited more favourable comparisons.

I was disappointed when I was not going to be travelling to Italy, as I really wanted to be on the pit road and on the front line of developments. I was to continue working in the factory, as there were 20 or so orders to be filled and the start of the racing season was only 6 weeks away. Nick told me I would be working on a development car in the factory, so that pleased me somewhat.

The car I was building was to be driven by an American driver, David Sturdy from Boston. He arrived at the factory with three of his mechanics, none of whom had any formal training in mechanics or car building. They said they were fast learners, but Jesus, they hadn't a clue.

The team members couldn't change a spark plug in a lawn mower. One was a hippy type and smoked marijuana, he was definitely chilled out enough to attempt anything new, but as for basic mechanical skills, he had none. I was supposed to show him how things were done, how the car was set up, show him how the dry sump system was plumbed, the cooling system layout, braking system and so on. He may as well have been looking into the space shuttle, such was his mechanical innocence.

I didn't mind, these guys were paying the bills and I was to get them to the grid at the first race of the season in Silverstone in late march. To say I was nervous was an understatement. David himself was a gentleman, who made his money in computers by all accounts, way ahead of his time, this was 1980 for god's sake and I had barely seen a computer by then.

Reports from Italy were not good. The car was two seconds off the pace of the previous year's car, despite the vast construction changes, and the wishbones broke under the strain. The car was deemed overweight also, and a professional test driver was employed, a Belgian driver, who was due to bring his own sponsorship to the team in the colours of Belga cigarettes. Thierry Tassin was his name, a proven driver with a good track record.

The damaged wishbones were sent back to the factory urgently for examination and modifications, then sent back to Italy for re-testing. Apparently, it turned out the car was a pig, despite frantic efforts to make it perform. It was sent back to the factory where an intensive weight saving session was carried out over a few days. The driver also suggested that the cars torsional rigidity was suspect as it was flexing too much, thereby making handling very unpredictable.

I was learning by the seat of my pants, very quickly. Once when I was grinding a burr off a magnesium upright, the whole thing reddened and caught fire in an instant. I reached for a container of water, only to add fuel to the fire. I didn't realise the water and magnesium were combustible, lesson learnt.

The weight saving methods were basic , they involved drilling huge holes in non stressed areas of the momocoque as well as cutting excess threads off any bolts in the car that were deemed too long. As regards the torsional rigidity, the car was placed on axle stands, and huge weights were attached to each corner of the chassis and dial gauges were placed on each corner to determine how much the chassis was flexing.

The solution was to radically alter the bulkheads front and rear, amongst other structural modifications. Poor Nick looked totally frustrated and exhausted by the long hours he spent trying to salvage the season before it even started. That poor man was definitely nearing burnout. An engine blew during one test session as a result of someone mistaking the oil pressure line for the suction line, five grand gone in a flash; there was murder in the camp.

I loved starting up the engines once everything was complete, the adrenaline flowed when I started to fill the magnesium dry sump oil tank, the sound of the engine, the smell off the brand new exhaust systems, when they would glow red with the heat after some time running, "Leave it ticking over for 10 minutes, then go up to 1500rpm for another 10, then to 2000rpm and up to 3500rpm", all the while looking out for temperature changes, oil pressure readings, any leaks detected, whilst making sure the electronics were functioning. It was with bated breath that everything was tickety boo; all was well with the car, I could relax.

I was staying in a nice flat in Thetford at the time and Nick told me there was a Japanese guy coming over to work and would I mind sharing the flat with him. I had no objections, and Kiyo arrived one day at the factory, all shy and raring to get stuck in at the deep end. Apparently, he had convinced Nick that he was the man for the job and was full of enthusiasm to get involved in F3 racing. He had a background in saloon car racing in Japan and was a fantastic worker, he could do anything he put his hand to, despite having pigeon English. He was very tidy too, which made living with him very conducive to a nice household.

Kiyo would get these huge food parcels from home with all types of Japanese delicacies, tea bags and sushi, noodles and more noodles. It was the equivalent to me getting bacon and cabbage I suppose, but he couldn't eat the English food. He was allergic to it.

We got on very well together, I used to drive to work in the mornings and we were both into going to race meetings nearby and in Silverstone circuit. I wanted to be a driver really, but this was my only way in, the next best thing, being a petrol head. I hadn't a notion of how to get sponsorship or anything like that, but I was just as happy with my own place for now. Nick had asked me during my interview whether I wanted to be a driver rather than a mechanic and I lied to him, of course I wanted to be a driver, but I had no driving experience in racing cars.

Lots of midnight oil later, and race day was approaching fast, the factory was a hive of activity and excitement, along with doubts about the cars potential. I too was nervous, as it was going to be my first race as team mechanic and I was fired up, but unsure of my own team's competence. They were complete amateurs and they thought it was going to be all fun and games during race day and qualifying. It was far from it.

It was very exciting to be in the pit lane in Silverstone for the first time. There were 23 cars qualifying for the race. Qualifying involved two sessions, an hour each, and a couple of hours apart. Before the qualifying officially started, drivers had a chance to give the cars a run for a few warm laps up before timed sessions. I had a quick look down the pit road, and there was Eddie Jordan, who ran the famous Jordan GP Team years later, going on to great success, he started out with a very professional F3 outfit at this time.

As the cars sat on the grid waiting for the first timed session, my heart was in my mouth, twenty or so cars doing lap after lap, occasionally coming into the pits for minor tweaks. My poor driver stalled the car as the flag went up to signal the first flying laps. It was embarrassing, as the other cars darted away in a spray of mist; David sat in the car waving his hands in the air. Thing didn't get much better later on, and he ended up on the back of the grid, about 2 seconds off the pace.

During the race, he got off the line ok, but he spun twice, a bolt broke in a rear wishbone and he came into the pits with the rear wheel hanging off at an acute angle. I frantically got a replacement fitted, but his race was run and the music stopped. He was not a happy camper, neither was his backroom team. Things didn't get much better for the remaining races, he was always at the back of the grid, even though the factory cars qualified well enough considering the uncompetitive nature of the car. No amount of lightening, modifying or tweaking this way and that worked. I suppose you can't make a race horse out of a donkey, as anyone in the horseracing industry will attest to.

I was getting fed up with the long hours and poor results, and as my first love was rallying, I packed up after three months working for Argo. I was a little home sick too, as there was no craic much in the old English villages at night. I missed Ireland and the Irish wit, so I went back to Dublin. ARGO drifted away from building F3 cars to building sports cars for the American Indy Lights series, amongst other projects, battered but unbowed.

I broke the news to Nick at the factory one morning and he left me go, he saw that I was a bit unhappy about living there. So I packed all my bits into my ford escort and drove to catch the ferry at Liverpool. After an hour or so, the exhaust in my car sprung a major leak, so I pulled up outside a small garage to get it welded. The car was on the ramp when the handbrake needed to be disengaged, so I climbed up on to the ramp to do the trick, and in my haste, I fell off the ramp on to the floor on the flat of my back. I couldn't move for a few minutes, I was in shock, but I got up and dusted myself down and recovered my composure.

When I was about an hour from the ferry terminal, the ignition light came on, the dynamo had packed up, but I had to keep going as I couldn't spend a night in Liverpool. I barely made it, I arrived at the departure ramp to find them lifting it up, so I blew the horn to get their attention and they allowed me on board with smoke billowing out from under the bonnet, I had broken the fan belt, the car was overheating and the battery was dead. I breathed a mighty sigh of relief on the boat.

My happiest years were spent working in Dublin in the early eighties, especially in Murphy and Gunn's in Rathgar. They were a bunch of comedians there and I loved the Dublin wit. We used to re- enact all sorts of scenarios in the workshop. I remember a great character by the name of Noel de Veasy. One day he dressed up as a Sheik with a turban around his head and a sheet wrapped around him. I would drive around Rathgar in a 735 BMW, pretending to be the chauffeur, whilst Noel was puffing a cigar and giving the royal wave out the back to anyone we encountered.

I laughed my arse off so many days there, it was fantastic. It was a privilege to work with those guys. It would have made great theatre. I often thought about writing a play based on the theatrics of that work environment, it was just a thought, along with thousands of others. I had no problems concentrating whilst working; I was totally absorbed by the job in hand, and gave it my all.

One particular day there was an army land cruiser in the workshop for a transmission build, and at some stage, Noel appeared with a driveshaft over his shoulder, mimicking a rocket launcher and we would hide behind cars in the workshop to dodge the fire, we laughed and laughed, and even Henry the service manager couldn't contain himself when he stepped out of his office for a moment. We were re-enacting a scene from the Lebanon, as the Irish Army had a peace keeping force there at the time.

Henry Freemantle, our service manager, had a great history in Motorsport. He built the fist turbocharged mini, which went on to win the British saloon car championship in the sixties with Alec Poole behind the wheel. He was a great character, a great engineer, who could build anything on wheels. He was lost in this hum drum environment of ordinary boring servicing and repair work, he was much too bright for that, but he had to survive too. I missed the challenging racing environment; I wasn't one for 9 to 5 jobs, but I couldn't have ended up in a better place in that regard.

When I came in to work the first morning, I was taking the cylinder head off a Toyota, and I was using an air ratchet, which speeded up the job considerably. Suddenly, I had an audience, as Nipper Kelly never saw one before and he was intrigued by this weapon. Needless to say, it wasn't long before that tool became the norm in the workshop. "That's some bleedin crown jewel you got there", was the reaction. It was so funny to see all the fuss over something so small. I must have increased the productivity by a quarter at least. I was really happy about that.

I had one very lucky escape in that garage. I was working under an old BMW 2002 replacing the clutch, when all of a sudden, the ramp collapsed on top of me with the car turning over on its side. I had run the opposite way and so I escaped injury or even death. I kicked the BMW in angst when I got out from under it whilst the lads in the workshop urged me to stay down on the ground and claim compo. Of course I got up straight away, that wasn't my mentality, I figured I was lucky to be alive. I was back to work in the afternoon.

Some of the antics we got up to were hilarious. On one occasion, I was working alongside another guy, nicknamed Lusty Lightening, when we played a prank with him. I wired up his tool box to the ignition system of a 735 BMW, started the car and asked Lusty could I borrow a spanner from his tool box. As he went to open the box he was suddenly hit by 10, 000 volts, was visibly stunned, but quickly walked away with his tail between his legs.

On another occasion, Nipper Kelly was fitting a rear differential on a Toyota Corolla k 30. As the diff could also be fitted upside down, he installed it incorrectly. He sat in the driver's seat and put the car into first gear when it jolted backwards. He discovered the car suddenly had 4 reverse gears and 1 forward, now that was very funny.

I still had the travel bug, I wasn't staying put for too long. I heard on the grapevine, that there was work in New York for mechanics. Though I had no green card, I bought a one way ticket in June '87. I had a cousin living in the Upper East Side, on 88THstreet, between second and third avenues. Before travelling, I had written a letter to Martin's Manhattan, a BMW dealer on the lower east side. He wrote back to me and said; "come on over", no problem here.

Of course I never mentioned that I had no green card, which was going to throw a spanner in the works. I arrived in JFK airport with a fresh face, innocent to the world, but dying to make an impact. I loved New York from the instant I arrived there, the brashness , the confidence, the intoxication of the city, the manic traffic, the sweltering humidity, the noise, the sound of the fire engines approaching , the yellow cabs like ants coming from all directions, the eccentricity of the people, the forthrightness of the people. What you saw was what you got with New Yorkers; they were very direct and didn't beat around the bush, unlike people at home.

One had to be on ones guard constantly, at first, never having experienced the likes of this huge city with its phenomenally high skyscrapers, and in particular, the Twin Towers, that icon of the American dream. It was invigorating, walking around the Downtown area, the senses were working in overdrive all the time, it was that good, and I was hooked. Everything was so convenient there; you could walk, take the underground, or jump in a cab, to move uptown or downtown with ease.

I strolled down to Martins Manhattan one Monday morning, to see if I could get work. I went in to the service manager's office and explained who I was and where I came from. He said there was no problem getting a job, just produce my green card. That caught me like a bolt out of the blue, I had no such thing and I told him the facts. He was very sympathetic, but stated that if I was found by Immigration officials, he would be fined thousands of dollars for employing an illegal immigrant.

I sheepishly walked out the door; I strolled around the lower east side and had a look around pier 57 and a couple of aircraft carriers, which were museum pieces on display. I figured that I had to do some cold calling later that day, and so I strolled around from garage to garage looking for work. Eventually, after making a few calls, I went up to east 84th street, just a few blocks from where I was staying, and I encountered a workshop called "Downtown Motors". There were a lot of German made cars there and I figured I might get a start here. I was lucky, and I was told to report for duty on the following Monday morning at 8am. Finally, I could relax for a few days and do a little sight seeing around the city, enjoy the free time I had left.

I also had to buy some tools as I could not bring them in through customs, as I was only here on a tourist visa. I organized for a friend in Dublin to send over my tool box by air freight, as tools were expensive, and weighed an awful lot. I asked a friend, Jackie, who worked in New York for 45 years or so, to drive me to JFK to collect the tools a week later. It was a bit of an epic, as the customs suspected that something was amiss here, but good old Jackie bluffed them into releasing the goods into his custody, after a considerable amount of badgering. I was relieved, as I was depending on my tools very much as I had only bought a skeleton set in Sears earlier in the week, and they would not suffice.

Jacky was one of the coolest individuals you could ever meet. He left Killarney when he was very young and emigrated to New York. He worked in the boiler room in Ward Island, which is a prison for the criminally insane, eventually retiring there and spending his time between New York and Killarney. The apartment we stayed in on the Upper East Side had been Jacky's weekend retreat, as he lived on Ward Island. He would come down to the city and go on the piss for the weekends and end up back in the pad snoring like a dinosaur until dawn.

The apartment on East 88th street was leased by a policeman for years and years, and when the policeman died suddenly, as he had no relatives, Jacky signed the lease in the policeman's name, thereby paying a nominal rent as he was employed by the city borough. When we would ring Jacky on Ward Island to see if he was coming down for the weekend, we would get an answering machine playing Irish music with the accompanying message; "I'm not in at the minute, but enjoy the music", I still laugh at the thought.

I started work on the Monday morning at 8 am, and it certainly was no picnic. This was June in New York with 90% humidity and temperatures in the 90's. There was no air-conditioning in the workshop, only one big fan; it was like a sweat shop. By 11am at break time, my shirt was wet from the humidity and I tried to relax with a bagel and coffee. The break was no more than ten minutes, when the manager urged us to get back to work, break time was over.

By lunchtime, I was really feeling the heat and counted the clock down until 1pm came. It was 1pm, not 12.55 or 12.56; they were relentless with the timing. If I even looked out from under the hood of a car, I was approached and told to keep my head down, it wasn't lunch time yet. This went on for three months before I had to quit in desperation, I was burned out from it. The only respite in the heat was to go to a bar or restaurant, anywhere with air conditioning.

Lester, the owner of this sweat shop, was a bit of a Chuck Yeager character, as he had served his time with the military in his early years. He also flew a small plane and had this girlfriend who was young enough to be his daughter. Not a week went by without me hearing about his weekend plans to fly away to some exotic destination; well it could have been Rikers Island for all I knew! He surely had some buddies up there!

It was my first time seeing closed circuit TV in a workshop, which was used to keep an eye on the workers, just in case you lifted your head up from under the hood of some weapon to take a breather.

I couldn't wait for Friday evenings to come, as the weekend beckoned, and we often drove to Jones's beach on Long Island to get away from the heat and humidity. Unfortunately, thousands of others had the same idea, and the drive took around two hours, torture in a car without air conditioning. It was great to lie on the beach, though the water was grey and murky, nothing like the pristine beaches at home.

It was hell for leather on the drive back to New York; we had to leave reasonably early in the afternoon before the other 20,000 cars. Driving on the freeways was very dull, eight lanes and not a hairpin in sight for miles, speed cops everywhere, very dull. But looking at some of the occupants of passing cars was fascinating, they were really a mixed bag, some hilarious looking pimp mobiles, limos and stretch Cadillac's all over the place. It shortened the journey somewhat.

When driving behind a car with New Jersey plates, you had to be very careful, as they would indicate to turn left, and then suddenly they would turn right at the last moment. You could see Manhattans s sky line in the distance, with its iconic Twin Towers standing above Manhattan, it was fabulous, and especially so at night, when it lit up like a Christmas tree. I loved walking up by the East River in the evenings, it was so calm and a nice breeze blew in from the sea.

Brunch on Sunday was my favourite day in New York, where we would regularly go to the same restaurant, as there was a waitress from Ballyhar, of all places, which is just a few miles from Killarney, working there, and she would give us extra portions of eggs and bacon. It was great sitting in the air conditioning and looking out on the street , where quite a few rollerbladers would pass by, going faster than the traffic. I wondered how they managed at a stop light, going at such speed. It epitomised for me the essence of the New Yorker, freedom to do unusual things, which were the norm over there. You would have been classed as insane doing the same stunts in Dublin at the time.

One Sunday afternoon, we went to Central Park to see the New York philharmonic orchestra in concert. The city mayor, Ed Koch, gave an address before the concert, to rapturous applause from the crowd. It was a carnival atmosphere; everyone had their own picnic baskets with exotic looking food and fine wines and champagne. It was so relaxed; you could hear a pin drop when the music started.

Central Park was a great place to spend an afternoon, lounging around in the sun, watching the roller bladders go on their slalom run, the impromptu American football played in groups, the joggers, who were running in 90 degree heat and humidity. I couldn't believe how they could do that. There was horse riding in the Park and even boating on the lake, not to mention the carriage drivers, many of whom were Irish.

My buddy, Chuck, worked pouring concrete in the high rise skyscrapers of Manhattan; he would be out at 6am and finish at 2pm. He got good money for that, and we would go to various bars and act like the glitterati, we were famous too! We spent most of what we earned, life was good.

In the evenings, we would go for a meal in lower Manhattan or The Village, where it was fascinating looking at all the different ethnic groups at the tables. There were the inevitable queues of people at the most popular restaurants and we would reserve a table for two in the name of "Murphy" on a regular basis. New York in the eighties was full of Irish immigrants, mostly illegal. They were dreading being caught by Immigration, and were very wary of going back to Ireland, as inevitably, they would be stopped by US officials at the airport and refused a re- entry visa. Lots of people went to extraordinary measures to get back in. Some came back via Canada or Mexico, usually crossed the border by road at some inauspicious crossing.

We decided to get away from the city one weekend and we borrowed an old Chevy from Jacky. He told us not to turn on the air conditioning as the car overheated. We set out for Boston, quite a distance away, and progress was slow, but we were in no particular hurry. It was nice driving through the countryside for once, getting out of the stifling heat and humidity. I now understood why the Glitterati moved to Long Island for the summer months, it was torture working in that heat, especially so in a job like mine.

We were motoring well until we pulled into a gas station to refuel. Another car was filling up and when he turned the ignition key, nothing happened, the battery was dead. We obliged him by salvaging jump leads from the trunk of the Chevy, but they were too light, and when we connected them, they fizzled and burned. Our battery gave up the ghost suddenly, and we were goosed.

What we didn't realise at this moment, an altercation was brewing between the other driver and the guy in the station. The driver produced a baseball bat and proceeded to attack the station employee with numerous blows. We were stranded in the middle of all this, as the car wouldn't budge. We pushed the car out of there as quick as we could, as we did not want to get involved in a fracas. Eventually we came across a garage and picked up a second hand battery to get us on our merry way. We arrived in Boston and stayed in a YMCA hostel for the weekend and had a lovely couple of days in the city. I loved Boston, something to do with their Irish heritage I'd say, the cops were great there, and they would set you right if you were in any difficulty whilst travelling.

It was back to the grindstone again on Monday morning; it reminded me of the days working in Harlesden, but without the tremendous heat. I liked driving around a few blocks of the city during a test drive; it was a relief from the relentless work and gave me a chance to take a breather. Driving was very stressful in the city, everyone seemed to be honking their horns relentlessly, if you hesitated at a traffic light for a milli second, they would blow you out of it. I enjoyed it though, I became one of them. It was no problem for me.

After three months, I decided to quit. That dreaded three month itch seemed to determine my working life, things got too familiar after three months, so I had to move on. I could take no more of the sweat shop environment. I had a look around for another job, but it was mostly the same old story. Any established dealer didn't want to know if you were working illegally, so the only prospect was working for some independent workshop where conditions were not as good.

I decided to go back home and see how things were going. At JFK check in, I placed my bag on the weighing scales and suddenly there was panic. It weighed 80 kilos, as it was full of mechanics tools. Police were called when the X-ray machine went ballistic, and I was called aside, frisked and questioned. It was only when they saw the tools that they realised I was no threat to anyone, except for the poor girl at the weigh in. She shrieked when lifting the bag and cried out in pain, arching her back a few times afterwards, I may have inadvertently dislodged a disc in her supine spine.

Before I went to New York, I had applied for a residency visa in Australia, but knew it would take a few months to process. I was only home for a couple of weeks when a letter arrived with my visa and work permit to Australia. I was delighted, as I felt restricted at home; I loved travelling, and especially going to new destinations. Australia always attracted me because of the great outdoors, the Irish heritage; it's fascinating history, its criminal connections, its outlaw tradition, with Ned Kelly being upmost in my mind, the Aborigine's in the vast outback, its varied wildlife.

I loved the idea of open spaces as far as the eye could see, the dry and dusty Nullarbor plain, the legendary mining towns like Kalgoorlie in the western desert, with its wild west connotations. Open spaces epitomised freedom to me, no matter where they were, but they were magnified a thousand times in Australia, a magnificent countryside, with endless opportunities for the explorer.

I came back to Dublin briefly, and worked for about three months in various garages, I was like an itinerant mechanic, but I loved the freedom of not being tied down to any particular employer for too long, I was a free spirit, and that's the way I wanted it to be. Whilst in Dublin, I bought a return ticket to Perth in West Australia. I figured it was a nice place to live, not too big a city, near the ocean, the desert, and the beautiful port city of Freemantle, which had just hosted The America's Cup yacht race.

In the departure lounge at Heathrow airport, I looked around and saw all these Aussies with their wide brimmed hats, sun burnt skin, the picture of contentment. I was coming from the relentless rain, westerly gales, depressed and stifled country, with too much church – state involvement, very restrictive and straight jacketed to my liking.

I liked the brashness of the Aussies, the confidence they had, believing it was the greatest country on the planet. I felt invigorated by their attitude. Ireland at this time was in a war, with the Border Fox Dessie O Hare, having just been killed in a shoot out with the Gardai. It was common news at home every evening, bombs going off under peoples booby trapped cars, subversives operating all over the country, especially North of the border, regular punishment beatings and murders. It would be interesting to look at it from far away.

I arrived in Melbourne at 8 am on a beautiful balmy morning, having spent 24 hours flying from London. I had a contact in Melbourne, a parish priest, who put me up for a few nights. I got the bus into the city to the sounds of Bob Dylan playing on the radio, it was really cool. Fr Tom proceeded to show me some of the sights around Melbourne. I was bleary eyed, and all I wanted was to bed down for a few hours somewhere, rather than being driven around almost comatose for hours on end. Melbourne was very cosmopolitan, it also had great weather, it was European like in lots of ways, the trams, the very clean streets, very pedestrian oriented. I liked it instantly.

Having spent a few days in Melbourne, I flew west to the city of Perth. Flying into the airport, I couldn't believe the amount of private swimming pools in the outskirts of the city. I got off the plane and it was shorts and tee shirt time again. It was a beautiful city, small but vibrant, very friendly.

I booked into a hostel in Hay Street in the City centre. It was very basic, but it was in the heart of the city, and everything was within walking distance, I loved it there. One thing I couldn't get used to was the cockroaches. They were always around, especially in the hostel, and inevitably, when trying to bunk down for a kip, I would hear the sound of cockroaches climbing around the room. Eventually, I took no notice of them, I liked being in the city so much, and I stayed there for 3 months.

At one stage, I looked for house sharing out in the suburbs, but only managed a couple of nights there, when I moved back in to the hostel. I missed the activity in the city, the company in the hostel, there were always interesting people passing through on their travels. One thing I didn't miss were the cockroaches, but they had a residency visa.

I scoured the newspapers looking for work, eventually made contact with an employer out on Scarborough beach road. Terry was a BMW dealer, and agreed to meet me in the city for an interview. He pulled up outside the hostel in his lovely M powered BMW and asked me a few questions about work experience and so on. Everything went well, and I started work in this lovely workshop on the second floor of this beautiful purpose built building. It had all the comforts, air conditioning, tinted glass for the intense sunlight coming through. It had a few Aussies as well as a few Kiwis working there; I was the only European, a novelty, I suppose.

Some of my fellow Aussie work mates were really impressed with my travelling CV, they wished to travel to Europe mainly, but America was really intriguing to them. Having come from working in the US, I could vouch for them that they were in the best country in the world at that time, with the stunning beaches, the laid back lifestyle, the gorgeous multi ethnic women, the availability of work anywhere in the country.

At the end of every month, the workshop was cleared and cleaned, in order to make way for a BBQ, with copious amounts of Tinnies and steaks on offer. All staff would attend these BBQ's and they were great, real Aussie stuff. There was a competition to see who could drink a Tinny the fastest, when they would puncture a hole in the bottom of the Tin before gulping it down in seconds. I challenged one macho sales guy to an arm wrestle, but he won, I lost 10 dollars. This was after all "Macho Man Country".

It was great working on the second floor of the building as we had a great view looking down on all and sundry. BMW were obsessed with their corporate image, and their sales staff seemed to be more like commodity traders, such was their demeanour. You could eat your lunch off the workshop floor it was so clean. Every morning it was cleaned and polished vigorously. Some of the guys would arrive at work having surfed on Scarborough beach that morning, which was only a couple of k's up the road. Boy, was that cool or what? I loved the freedom and the open spaces, the fabulous beaches, the laid back attitude.

I loved driving the M Powered BMW's on road tests; I didn't want to go back to the workshop, so I would drive for half an hour on occasions when a very special car arrived for servicing. It reminded me of working in London when I drove the jaguar XJ 12's in a frenzy of rubber smoke, but the weather was more conducive to warming the tyres.

On one occasion, the service manager asked for a volunteer to take the cylinder head off an M powered 6 series BMW, as the other staff were reluctant to go at it. I took the cylinder head off and brought it to the machine shop in order to plane it. I was making great progress and I had everything assembled after half a day, when I went to start the engine; Clunk; it was seized solid. I had to take it all apart again and I discovered that the head gasket I was using was a different sized bore, as this engine had been over- bored to increase volumetric capacity. Red faces all round, but I had it going later on that day

The West Australian believed he was superior to the rest of the nation. When I was interviewed for the job, one of the first questions was; "Had I worked in WA before"? They lived in the knowledge that this was the greatest place on earth, and they weren't far out. There was a smugness about them, and I envied that in certain ways, but having just come from New York, it was no surprise to me. I had gained a lot of confidence during my travels; it was great to see somewhere new and fresh.

One night, I was watching the news on television, when live coverage was beamed of two undercover police officers coming upon the funeral of an IRA man in the North of Ireland. The mourners proceeded to attack the occupants of the unmarked car and dragged them out the windows and beat them to death. I squirmed while I watched, I was ashamed to be Irish at that moment, and I curled up in my chair in disbelief. What would the Aussies think of this utterly repulsive act of savagery? It was very disturbing, and I was upset having seen this coverage, as I'm sure were most people in the civilised world. I was upset for weeks afterwards and kept a low profile.

I got friendly with a Japanese girl whilst in Perth, Takako was her name. I met her in the street where she was handing out fliers one morning and we hit it off instantly. We would go out to Scarborough beach frequently on the bus and had great banter between us. She was going out with an Irish guy at the time and they intended to go back to Japan and settle down. I loved the Japanese people, so gentle and kind; they exuded an air of graciousness and dignity. They were very interested in the politics of Ireland, but nearly everyone thought the civil unrest and IRA violence went on south of the border as well as the North. It was difficult to give a reasonable explanation for the troubles, as the outsider had no idea of the North – South divide. As far as most people were concerned, Ireland was a war zone.

I went to dinner in the homes of some of my work mates and the conversation inevitably turned to the troubles in Ireland, and the other topic was the amount of Irish people in Australia and around the world. They wondered was anyone at home at all? Who was running the country? It was with a heavy heart, when I left Ireland, as I'm sure lots of people will attest to. But once I got away, I was happy with my lot, though homesick for a while.

I eventually moved out to the suburbs, and shared a house with an Italian and an Australian couple. The Italian guy turned out to be a male escort, and I was surprised at that. It was only after a few weeks, that I noticed he was on the phone an awful lot, and the conversations were racy to say the least. This guy certainly had no hang ups, he boasted regularly about the number of women he had regular contact with and they would pay him up to 300 dollars for taking them out to dinner and afterwards to a hotel for rampant sex. I wished that I had the same confidence that John had.

John was a fruit seller by day and would be out at 6am every morning to go to the market. He was a real Italian Stallion, full of macho behaviour. It was only when he got a pit bull, that I was concerned for my safety, as the dog barked all night and would attack any dog in the street with ferocious vigour. This went on for a couple of weeks before the dog was discarded, as he was causing havoc in the house and the neighbourhood. John apologised for the behaviour and was a proper gentleman afterwards.

Women at that stage were an after thought; I was more concerned with cars and gaining work experience. I always loved interacting with women, especially foreign women. Perth was a very liberal city, it was my first time seeing transsexuals and lady boys walking around with no fear of intimidation, it was accepted as normal. I had to look twice at first as I couldn't believe my eyes, even at 10 am in the morning they were walking down the street dressed to kill. I admired their brashness, their disregard for convention.

I used to get the train to Freemantle in the evenings and I would stop off at some beach and go for a swim in the lovely warm waters with tremendous surf rolling in, it was really refreshing after the heat of the day. I particularly liked going to Swanbourne beach as it was a nude beach and the women were stunning looking. Whilst in Freemantle, I made contact with the parish priest, Fr Hanna, whose name I had got in my travels across Australia. He showed me his beautiful church and I was feted one afternoon, gorging myself on liquorice sweets and nuts amongst other exotic fruits. He gave me a tour of the lovely church and he played a CD of church music at full volume in the empty church, I think he was showing off, but I wasn't impressed by the display.

I was getting homesick at various stages, and as I had a return ticket, I would go to the travel agent and book my return trip on numerous occasions, only to cancel it a few days later. I missed Dublin, in particular, as I had fond memories of the place and its people. I would ring home on various occasions, only to get the same response; "There's nothing here for you, stay out there".

Ireland was a somewhat desolate place in the eighties, not much in the way of opportunity, despite my willingness to work hard, no matter where I went. Hard work to me equalled satisfaction, purpose, stimulation, reward, achievement. I never considered going on the dole, ever. I was too proud, and I figured if I was able to work, then why waste your time laying about. I had seen too many people wasting their lives away, bumming around, going to pubs and betting offices, having no purpose in life. I dreaded ending up like that and I was determined to keep working, no matter what.

I would have felt guilty taking a day off at any stage; I suppose I was programmed in a certain way. I was a dream employee, I never shirked at a problem, I jumped straight in and dug deep, even though it didn't always work out in the end. My work rate was relentless, and I followed it up with many mountaineering trips and mountain biking with the same intensity. I was an avid admirer of Reinhold Messner and he's tremendous solo ascents of treacherous Himalayan peaks, death defying in many instants. I loved his drive, his work ethic, his focus, and laterally the exploits of Tom Crean from Annascaul, the unassuming hero of Antarctica all those years ago.

Extreme sports of any kind attracted me. I was an adrenaline freak, thought nothing of climbing two or three mountains in the morning and biking in the afternoon. I could never get enough of it, until I fell exhausted into bed later that night. If I got injured for any period, I would be down in the dumps, as I figured I wasn't smart enough to avoid injury. Of course, that was complete nonsense, as at the rate I was going, it was impossible to avoid injury or accidents. It was like the great Ari Vatanen's mantra; "if you don't crash, then you are not trying hard enough", I lived like that for years, never took the easy option. I tortured myself if I hadn't put in an honest effort in anything I did.

I decided to come back home in the spring of '88, having spent almost a year in Australia. I wasn't totally happy about leaving, as I knew from experience, that this was a great place to live, tremendous outdoor activities, fantastic beaches, laid back lifestyle, but the old Irish psyche kicked in; "this is too good to be true" , I must get away from here to realise how good it has been.

I arrived back in Heathrow 24 hours later to a damp cloudy day. I was frozen with the cold and my first reaction was; "what the fuck am I doing back here"? with all these people dressed in full winter attire. I was not looking forward to going home at that stage. I knew then that I should have stayed longer and travelled a bit more around Australia. I arrived back in Dublin and took the bus into the city, which looked like a total kip compared to any planned Australian city, derelict buildings all over the place, damp dreary days, dreadful traffic jams, a horrible looking place coming from my perspective.

The first thing I did when I got into Dublin was to buy a return ticket to Australia. There was no way I was going back to the future. I stayed in Dublin for a few nights, in a bed and breakfast, even though I had some family members living there.

I hated the coldness of the place, the dark dreary nature of the city. I went back home to Killarney after a few days and tried to settle in somewhat. As my mum was not well at the time, I felt obliged to stay at home and look after her, as everyone else in the family were getting on with their lives, mostly in Dublin. I felt like a loose cannon around the place, too much time on my hands, no stimulation, coming back to a depressed economy, and more depressing weather.

However, I persisted, and after three months, I decided to go on a start your own business course with Fas, which went on during the winter months of '88/'89. I found it to be very monotonous, drawn out, uncomplicated. I just wanted to go back to work, for god's sake. I was programmed to work; I wasn't one for hanging around, killing time. I felt very restricted at home, coming back into this situation, where I had no alternative but to stay and help out. The idea of going back to OZ was hit on the head big time now.

In the back of my mind, I always had an inkling of going back to Kalgoorlie in the desert, as one could live there in a tin shed for very little. It was a mining town, and appealed to me as I could have found work there easily, and I could have lived comfortably there for very little. Kalgoorlie, to me at the time, had similarities with the Klondike gold rush of the early 19th century. I loved reading about that whilst in my leaving certificate year in st Brendan's in Killarney. I loved in particular, the epic journeys through the snowy mountains in Montana, and the hardship endured by those hardy individuals.

By the end of the Fas course, I was chomping at the bit, willing to work. I found a small workshop in Killarney town and started organizing it and fitting it out. It was slow progress; everything seemed to be happening in slow motion, too slow for me, too mundane. I wanted much more, considering where I had come from. I needed much more activity and stimulation.

Ireland was a desolate place at the time, no jobs, no prospects, all doom and gloom, even the weather man looked depressed. At least the weathermen in Australia cracked a joke at the end of their announcements, here in Ireland, they looked straight jacketed, compliant, gloomy, in comparison to their Australian counterparts. The weather was not much better either. I tried my best to make my workshop bright and airy. In retrospect, I was fighting a losing battle. At the time in Ireland, everyone was obsessed with getting on the property ladder, empire building. Bending over backwards to please the bank manager, kiss his arse, play to the gallery, get ahead of the pack, get recognised, it was all perception.

I had come back from the land of plenty, to the land of sorrows and negativity, choked by church and state influence, stunted by corporate greed, milked dry by avaricious public servants. Any man in his right mind would never go into self employment at the time, if he was smart, he could have lobbied his local politician and blended into a harmless civil service job. All he had to do was; "be in on time, leave on time, and take his time", no sweat. I was not going down that road; I hated that scenario from the start, me being a maverick.

Eventually, I managed to get started, it seemed to take months to get things organised, and it was laboriously slow. I missed the Australian outlook, their laid back nature, the beautiful weather, but I was back home so shouldn't I be happy? I felt removed and disconnected from reality. I was still living in Australian mode, trying to replicate it here on my own. Everyone seemed so serious and pre-occupied. I felt like an outcast, but I tried to blend in. Most of my family were either teachers or public servants; they lived independently away from home, whilst I felt obliged to stay and look after my parents, as well as trying to establish myself in business. I put myself under a lot of pressure, taking on too many jobs at once, and trying to bring perfection into the equation. I was a slave to myself, never satisfied with the job in hand. I could always have done a better job in my own mind.

I became very active by cycling and mountaineering to a very high level in the early 90's. It was a great stress reliever for me, and I loved the solitude of the outdoors, I felt at home in that environment. Not a week went by when I would have run up and down three or four mountains and cycled another 30 miles or so afterwards. No gully was steep enough or wet enough for me, the harder, the better, I was a natural athlete. I craved adrenaline, the highs were intoxicating.

If I were a drug addict at the time, heroin would have been my sauce, nothing less would suffice. I always looked at my watch at the end of a mountain run or cycle, to see if I had bettered my previous time, aiming to go faster on the next outing. This went on relentlessly. It was the same at work, I would have the days work finished by lunchtime. It gave me the opportunity to get on the bike or out on the hills for numerous hours in the afternoon, especially in the summer months.

Chapter 2

ILLNESS

In June 1990, I was climbing Howling Ridge on Carrauntuohill, when I noticed the ground moving when I looked back down from the ridge. I felt very strange, something was not right. I brushed it off and dismissed it as a fever or something, and carried on up the mountain. I made the summit and rested for a while. As I descended, whilst jumping from boulder to boulder, I knew my co-ordination was not what it should have been. A couple of days later, I was cycling on the Kenmare road when I found it difficult to balance the bike, and I felt moments of vertigo. I was getting worried now, as it was not getting better, and I was getting weaker. When walking up the street, I had to stay in by the wall or shops as I was beginning to stagger like a drunk, I couldn't walk the line.

I went to my doctor, who diagnosed vertigo and put me on motilium for a couple of weeks and said to come back by then and he would see how I was doing. I was not getting any better, and my energy levels were dropping drastically, my balance was getting worse, and I was feeling sick regularly as well. I couldn't wait two more weeks, so I went back to my doctor, who suggested having a neck x-ray.

Another week went by before the results of the x-ray came back, and the doctor noted from the radiologists report that there were signs of arthritis on my neck, that could explain my symptoms. I was completely baffled, and was at the doctor's mercy. I knew in my heart and soul it had to be something more serious. I was literally falling into bed with exhaustion at this stage, could not walk straight, feeling constantly faint, and on top of that, I felt weakness down my right arm, stroke like symptoms, with my speech also slurring.

It was very serious now, and I was very concerned for my well being. I lost confidence in my doctor, and asked him to refer me to another physician. I drove over to Tralee to my appointment with this Physician, in my weakened state. I could barely walk in to his waiting rooms. The physician sat me on the bed and did a few basic neurological tests, dimmed the lights and shone a flashlight into my eyes whilst I looked to the ceiling and then down to the floor. He also got his little hammer and tested my reflexes by knocking the ball of my knees and elbows. He looked as baffled as I did. I asked him what he thought, but he was non committal, barely spoke at all. He did ask me if I'd ever had a brain scan, to which I replied; "No Sir". He recommended getting a brain scan urgently and sent me back to Doc Holiday, my own doctor.

My GP said that he would write to the hospital to arrange an appointment for a brain scan that week, no rush of course, I was still breathing. I couldn't believe what I was hearing, here I was, falling over myself, disintegrating before his eyes and he writes to the hospital for an urgent appointment! That would take another week or so.

Four weeks had now elapsed since my symptoms began and I was getting no answers. I was still working at this stage, and carried on until one day, I went to push start a customer's car and I collapsed in a heap on the road. I got the car going all right, but I was left flat on my back on the road for a short while. It was then, under extreme pressure, that my doctor was forced almost at gun point to get a bed for me in the Mercy hospital in Cork. I had nothing left, was constantly feeling faint, the life was draining out of me.

I remember a nun in the admissions office asking me whether I had health insurance or not. When I replied; "no I have none," She retorted; "this could cost you a fortune". That was the last thing on my mind; I was more concerned with my diagnosis, and feared for my life. The first night I was put into a ward with eight beds, filled mainly by elderly patients, some of whom had varying stages of dementia amongst other ailments. One particular individual had an oxygen mask over his mouth and cried out constantly; "I'm dying, I'm dying".

There was no more than three feet between beds, and it was very disturbing to witness first hand this entire trauma. I couldn't sleep for one minute that night, with the constant wailing and weeping. It was very distressing. In the middle of the night, a traveller was brought into the ward, comatose from alcohol, and placed in a bed with guard rails around it. He kept pulling off the rails and falling out on the floor. A nurse eventually settled him, but by that stage, I was out of it, totally exhausted and mentally traumatised by the whole scenario. I said to the nurse that I couldn't spend another night there, as I had nothing left inside me, I couldn't cope with it. She got me a twin bedded room for the following night and it was like heaven compared to the first night.

A nurse took a blood sample from me and I fainted promptly, sweating profusely. She asked me was I squeamish at the sight of blood being drawn, but it was more to do with my weakened state, rather than the sight of blood. I went back to bed afterwards and tried to rest. My mind was working in overdrive, trying to imagine the endless possible commutations of the surgery that seemed inevitable to me.

I was eventually given a number of cat scans over a few days, and one morning a doctor approached my bed with the devastating news; "You have a Haema-Angioblastoma in the Posterior Fossa of your brain". I was shattered by the news, even though I was unsure of what it was, but it sounded very serious indeed. I broke down in front of the nurse and asked her was I going to die? She tried to reassure me, and calmed me somewhat, but I was grief stricken.

I was in the Mercy hospital for 5 nights and was transferred to CUH for further scans and imminent surgery later in the week. As the August weekend was approaching, I knew the surgical staff would be off for the weekend, as only emergency surgery would be performed, and my case was no emergency by all accounts. On the Friday of the August weekend I was lying in my bed when the neuro surgeon came around with his team to observe me. I felt like a monkey in the bed. I asked him was it ok if I went home for the weekend as I was starving with the hunger, the hospital food was crap and I was living on honey crisp bars. He said it was ok, to stay in bed at home and report for surgery on Tuesday morning, coming back on the Monday evening. I rang home to get someone to collect me, and they were rather stunned at my request. I wanted to get out of the hospital environment for the weekend, regardless of the consequences.

When I arrived home, I was relieved, to get a proper meal firstly, and to just lounge around from bed to kitchen. Some woman brought a cooked chicken to our house, and I proceeded to devour it like an animal, using my fingers, such was my hunger. I even managed to go to Kate Kearney's Cottage for a pint on the Sunday. I had to use a walking stick for support, as my balance was gone almost totally, but that pint tasted better than anyone before. It was a beautiful sunny August weekend, all the tourists were out in the summer sun, relaxing and enjoying the scenery. I milked every second, as I did not know what to expect the following week in hospital. I was scared, and felt helpless and vulnerable. I wished for a brief moment, that I could relax here and have another pint and chat with people, but my mind was pre-occupied with the road ahead.

I survived the weekend and arrived back in hospital on Monday afternoon. I collapsed into bed, totally spent, worried about my survival. There was a last minute hitch that night as the surgeon who was supposed to operate on me was not available, so a Jordanian neurosurgeon whom I had never even met, was due to operate on me in the morning. I was looking forward to getting it out, whatever it was, and going back to some semblance of an independent life again. I realised the dangers involved in the surgery, particularly any brain surgery, and I was prepared for the worst. I didn't expect to function as well as I had before the surgery. That scared the hell out of me, but I accepted the risks. I had no choice.

After six hours of surgery, I was wheeled into intensive care. I was semi-conscious; my head was pounding with excruciating pain. I found it hard just to lift my head off the pillow, the pain was indescribable. I have no recollection of leaving intensive care, or going back to the ward, it was all a blur to me. I came around at one stage when the surgeon looked in on me, but my motor function and reactions were very slow. Apparently, I had developed blood clot; so on the following morning I was wheeled down to surgery again, re-opening the same wound at the back of my head.

I somehow survived, and woke up in a total daze, bewildered, very sore, with double vision now also. I had a bed by a window and I tried several times to stand up whilst holding on to the radiator nearby, but I couldn't support myself. I looked down at my legs, and they were just skin and bone, all the muscle had wasted away, after three weeks in bed. It took an enormous effort to take a few steps with the aid of a walking frame. After a few paces, I was fit to fall back into bed again, shattered. Progress was excruciatingly slow and painful. In the mornings, I would take a few steps down the corridor and then fall back into bed. I was taken down to the gym a few mornings later, and a nurse proceeded to throw a ball at me to test my reflexes. This was crazy, as I was in no shape for goalkeeping duties. I thought it was highly inappropriate considering my state; it was difficult enough just to stand up, never mind dart across the room.

I was progressing well and I was looking forward to going home, however remote the possibility seemed, but once I could walk and the wound in my head was healing, then I figured I could make a stride to get out of there. I was determined to go home and when I suggested to the consultant that I was fit to go home, he didn't hesitate, and off I went, in a wheelchair, as I couldn't manage to walk the considerable distance to the car.

On the drive home to Killarney, I found the sunlight very painful, as any sort of bright light pained my eyes. I was glad to get back home, and could only manage to lie down in the darkness for days on end, in total silence. I hated any noise, it irritated my senses, which were very sensitive to sound and light. I managed to go out in the garden with a walking frame some days later, and took baby steps with great care.

Another couple of weeks and I was able to walk unaided, but only just. I ventured into town a couple of times, but I found it very difficult to navigate between pedestrians, my reactions were very slow and laboured. I had to avoid the town eventually as I couldn't handle the traffic on the footpaths. Walking a straight line was the best I could do, the path of least resistance.

A couple of months passed and eventually I was walking with ease, getting into my stride, though when on rough ground I found it very difficult to change direction quickly. It took six months before I could get my confidence back and venture into the mountains again. I attempted to climb Carrauntuohill one day, but turned around at the first level, only one third of the way up. I was happy just to be out on the hill again. I missed it so much, it had become routine for me, as regular as having breakfast. I lived for the adrenaline of running up and down mountains, it was no good sauntering along, I would have to be pumping sweat and straining muscles in order to get the best out of it.

I was returning to fitness by December 1990, when one day I noticed I was weakening again, my stomach was sick, my balance was poor, and my double vision was getting worse. I made an appointment with my surgeon, and he sent me for a cat scan. My worse fears were confirmed a few days later when I spoke to the surgeon. He told me the root of the tumour was still there, it hadn't been removed fully.

I was devastated, and concerned. It was only the 8th of December and he sent me home to rest and come back for more surgery on January the 15th. I was getting sick three or four times daily for the month of December, and I was losing weight at an alarming rate. I had no energy whatsoever, and spent my time lying down or throwing up in the bathroom. I really didn't think I would make it until the January deadline. I just wanted the pain to stop, I was prepared for death.

By January the 14th, I was barely able to walk out to the car, for the journey to Cork. I had to take a plastic basin with me as I was getting sick constantly, and on a couple of occasions, the car had to pull over so I could get sick. I didn't understand how I was constantly throwing up as I was unable to eat anything for fear of getting sick, my stomach was in a rancid state, it took so much energy just to get sick that I was shattered.

I was glad to be admitted to a ward in the hospital, I crumpled up in a ball in the bed, after being wheeled into the ward. I couldn't lift my head off the pillow; I was wasted, on deaths door. A doctor gave me an injection for the sickness, and it helped a little. I thought I would die that night, I was in such pain.

If ever there was such a thing as out of body experience, I certainly had one that night. I remember being in a place where there was absolute peace and contentment, no pain whatsoever, a profoundly spiritual experience, it had to be heavenly, I was convinced. It was like an angel was beside me, trying to convince me that it would be ok, either way. I would survive, if not, I would go to a better place.

The following morning I was wheeled down to the operating theatre, and I started to throw up whilst waiting on the trolley outside. A doctor approached me and said that soon it would be all over, the pain, the sickness, the overwhelming anxiety. I wanted closure either way, whatever that entailed. The anaesthetist administered her injection to sedate me and I was on my way.

A few hours passed when I groggily came round in the recovery room, oxygen mask over my face, in incredible pain. I was getting such a high dose of antibiotics and pain killers that all I could taste in my mouth was the drug infusion. I could feel them going down every inch of my throat, that sickening feeling, and into my stomach, which was by now unable to function due to toxic contamination. I continued on getting sick several times daily, couldn't take food of any sort, and was getting dehydrated and comatose as I wasn't taking in enough fluids. I attempted to get out of bed one morning, and I just about managed to take a few steps unaided. This was partly due to my earlier fitness regime, leading up to my latest surgery. I shudder to think what may have happened had I not been fit going into the hospital.

The morning of my surgery was the 15th of January 1991. That was the morning the Gulf war erupted as a result of Iraq invading Kuwait. One of the doctors at the time was named Mr Aziz, and the prime minister of Iraq at the time was Tariq Aziz. It was the first time I can remember that live footage of a war was covered by CNN and other networks. It was fascinating to see the aerial bombardments of Iraq, it was like play station, but little did we know about the suffering it caused to the poor people of Iraq.

I had my own suffering to cope with and I was facing a long road to recovery. Its funny some of the details of that war I remember, specifics, like the new weapons the US would use, for example the Daisy Cutter, a bomb designed to penetrate bunkers and maximise causalities. I remember vividly the burning oil wells in the Kuwaiti desert, the legendary Texan Red Adair, employed to plug the leaking oil wells, the intense acrid smoke, and the salvage teams covered in oil trying to do their job. It was like reality TV. It was total Apocalypse if ever there was one. Desert Storm may as well have been a computer game, with swashbuckling general Norman Schwartzkoff, the big American hero, deployed to sort out the insurgents in the stifling heat of Kuwait.

What kept me focussed in all this recovery was an E type jaguar, above all things. I had been restoring an old jaguar at the time and I wanted to get back working again, if at all possible. I would dream of driving on a sunny day with the hood down, the wind in my face, the smell of the lovely leather upholstery, the sound of that lovely straight six engine, the clunk in the diff when you changed gears, a real driver's car, no fancy electronic aids, and no power steering, great for building up the biceps. It was a labour of love, no doubt about it. I could smell that leather from my hospital bed. I could imagine the needle in the rev counter climbing gradually, all the gauges, lovely analogue devices working temperamentally, a bit like myself.

Two weeks after the operation, I walked unaided out of the hospital to a waiting car. I felt happy about walking out on my own, though I was in excruciating pain. I could function well enough to gain some form of independence. The hardest part of my recovery was the constant sickness that would go on for another year, until it finally settled. If you cannot eat, then you won't gain any strength, and that was how it worked for the next few months. The pain in my head lasted for another 6 months or so, my double vision remained the only permanent legacy of my surgery, but I lived with it. It could have been much worse. I counted my lucky stars, prayed for strength to come back, to enable me to do all those things I had taken for granted over the years.

Six months later, I was back climbing mountains, though slowly, nothing compared to my previous ramblings. I made it a regular routine, maybe twice a week at first, and then increasing the pace gradually and started back cycling as well. One week I climbed Carrauntuohill six times in seven days, it was then I decided I was ready to go back to work. I had spent two years and three months getting back to normal, and I wanted to get back into a working routine.

I went back to work in the spring of 1992, though I was advised by my surgeon to take up something easier, less demanding physically. I was having none of that, I was a mechanic, first and foremost, and I loved the work. I never considered having a desk job or anything like that; I couldn't stay seated for half an hour in any one place, I had to work at this job, I trained for it and worked very hard at it. It was a no brainer. What else was I supposed to do? Is the Pope a catholic? Does Dolly Parton sleep on her back?

This was Ireland in the early nineties, a fairly depressed place economically, no jobs much, slim prospects. I was never academically minded, hated going on any kind of course, being confined in a room all day when I could be out on the bike or up a mountain somewhere or swimming across a lake. ! And so it was, I was back where I wanted to be.

I was glad to get back into a work routine again. I didn't feel fulfilled or complete without having a job to go to. I was a very driven person in every way, demanded way too much from myself, tortured myself with the idea of perfection, nothing was ever good enough, I could always do better. Every couple of months, I would return to hospital to have a cat scan to see how my recuperation was going. I was always worried about the possibility of a recurrence, but as time went by, it was just a routine thing. It was always a nervous time, going back to the consultant, to read the scans. I often considered the consequences of a recurrence, the painful surgery, the long recuperation, and the endless possibilities.

Cork City became synonymous with hospital visits, pain, more pain, sickness, after the endless journeys over the county bounds. For many of these journeys, I had to bring my sickness container with me and the driver would have to pull over even in the middle of the street in order to let me puke my stomach contents up onto the road. Any sudden movements made me throw up, especially in the passenger's seat. As soon as I got my results from the consultant, I jumped straight in the car and headed for home, as I knew I wouldn't survive the journey without getting sick. At first, I was not allowed drive, because of my double vision, and it took about six months before I would get behind the wheel again. I was a very lucky man.

I started back cycling, mountaineering, and swimming, at my previous pace, but more intense, as I figured it may not last, enjoy it while I can. I wanted to blend in again seamlessly, go about my business quietly. I always hated being in the limelight for any reason. I would avoid it like the plague. I just wanted to put my head down and tear into an engine or gearbox and rip it apart. I always made sure it was put back better than it was originally, otherwise I would berate myself for not getting it right. The same was true whilst out on a mountain, I tortured myself if I had failed to put in the ultimate effort. I was my own worst enemy. Whilst working in Murphy and Gunn's in Dublin we used to try and stand a 50 pence coin on the cam covers of BMW engines to see who had the built the smoothest running engine, if the coin stayed upright at idle speed, it was perfect.

I used to walk with Killarney Mountaineering Club at this time, as I was out in the mountain so often, I would invariably come across them, up some gully or ridge. It was a way of getting to know like minded people, if there was such a thing. I was a natural at this anyhow, no amount of storms or bad weather kept me off the hill. I looked forward to the weekend walks with relish, as I loved roaming the mountains, no restrictions, just me and the weather and sometimes impossible looking ground, but invariably, I'd find a way through.

There were regular trips abroad to the greater ranges, the Alps, trekking in Nepal, South America, and ski trips in various resorts. It was intoxicating, life involved just surviving between trips away, adrenaline fuelled junkets you could call them. We partied hard during these trips also, inevitably drinking till all hours, staggering out of nightclubs and pubs, only to rise early the following morning to repeat the process.

One Sunday morning, in March 1992, when I drove down to our meeting point for the club walks, there was a Canadian lady waiting to join the group walk. She mentioned that she had walking experience in the Canadian Rockies, and that she was fit enough. Apparently, she had come to Ireland because she had become stressed out with her life back in Vancouver, so with the help of a friend of her family, a presentation nun, she got a job working voluntarily with Kerry Parents and Friends in Killarney, who help children with downs syndrome and other disabilities. She was a highly trained teacher back in Canada, spent her time driving from school to school in the Prairie Provinces, helping children with learning difficulties, a special needs teacher you could call it here at home, they were known as Mentally Challenged in Canada. Sure aren't we all?

She had some kind of breakdown, and she was very intense at the beginning, it took her a long time to relax into the Irish way of life. She seemed different to other women; she was very smart and intuitive. She loved getting out in the mountains, the craic in the pub afterwards, the Irish wit, the banter. It was as if she had a sheltered life back in Canada. She was also a very talented artist, her detail was mind boggling, her focus was total, in whatever she did. I was attracted to her, eventually. I loved her enthusiasm, the way she saw things in people that nobody else twigged, her passion for her work, her love of the outdoors and the Kerry air.

We became friends, would cook dinner in her house, have people over, and laugh and joke all night long. She would sing and loved Irish dancing and Irish music. Her enthusiasm was infectious, her compassion was great, her attention to detail second to none. We would go away for weekends to places like Allihies in West Cork, and she loved the accents of the locals in the pubs, she laughed at their many sayings, their lovely gentle nature. She was able to put into words exactly how to describe different personality traits in people just by observing their nuances.

As time went by, I fell hopelessly in love with Karen; it all came together one sunny weekend on a club walk around Glanmore Lake in South Kerry. We stayed in the hostel in that lovely picturesque magical wonderland. I noticed that Karen was sitting outside in the morning sunshine, studying hard, as she was working on some tutorial or other. I used to get up early and join her outside the hostel, and I would laugh and joke with her, telling her to drop the study for the weekend, it was so beautiful there. She joined me for a walk down by the lake and we spoke about life and our wishes in this world. She mentioned that she didn't want any "complications", that being yours truly!

However, I had other ideas, she wasn't going to get out of it that easily, and so it went.

After the club walk, we drove down to Killmac for pints, and we took a stroll down the pier together and instantly, we seemed to hit it off, I kissed her on the wall by the pier, I loved her from that moment on! I didn't want to leave her side.

Karen often mentioned that she wanted to go on to further studies and mentioned numerous times her intention to go to Goldsmiths College in London to study Art – Psychotherapy. She had gone to London for interviews and to check out the college.

As she was a non national in Ireland, she was not allowed to work for profit, so any money she got, she earned from tuition on the side, and her mother supported her from back home in Canada.

It was with a bomb shell when she announced that she would be taking her place in Goldsmiths College, after nearly two years in Killarney. I was devastated that she would be leaving, and thought she may never come back. The course was normally of 4 years duration, but she convinced them that she could do it in two years, as she could not afford to spend 4 years in London, as her mother was paying most of the cost.

I dreaded the thought of her leaving, I even considered moving to London to support her and work there again. She wouldn't have it, as she wanted to concentrate on her studies and didn't want any distractions. It was going to be very tough, doing a four year course in two years, with very intensive psychotherapy sessions thrown in regularly. It was mind boggling. I was heartbroken when she left.

I kept in touch with her by letters, I must have written at least ten letters a week for the first year of her course. She loved having Killarney as her escape from the coldness of London. She hated London with a passion, never seemed to warm to the place.

I made a trip to London once a month, to help her through her orientation process, and I also made sure she got back to Killarney at least once a month. I would leave a pre paid airline ticket at the check in desk in Heathrow, to make it easier for her, as money was always tight.

We used to joke about all the executives on board the flights to London, with their pin striped suits and pale faced skin and clutching their brief cases as if the crown jewels were enclosed, whilst we were sun burnt and weather beaten form lots of outdoor activities and were totally relaxed.

Despite her contempt for London, she really managed to enjoy the weekends when I was over there; we visited art galleries and museums, went to pubs in the West End and walked around the beautiful parks in the city. We would also go to the many markets on Saturday mornings, taking the bus into town. We also witnessed the changing of the guard at Buckingham Palace, we laughed at how they could keep their composure in the summer heat, especially with so many people going out of their way trying to distract their eyes from the robotic stare they had.

We went shopping in Oxford Street, and when we were in a clothes store, there was a very long queue for the changing room, so I urged her to get on with it and try on whatever garment she wanted outside the changing room. So she gets a knickers and proceeds to put it on over her jeans in protest, to the astonishment of a big black woman who laughed her heart out at the sight of it, it certainly broke the ice, we all laughed together.

The study was getting increasingly frantic, it was very demanding on her emotionally, but she was very determined to see it through, not to lose face, and she was very conscious of the short time line.

One project she had to do involved going into prisons in London and interviewing criminals and psychopaths in order to gain an insight into their motivations, their mind set. This really unhinged her as she was threatened with violence on numerous occasions, and she did not foresee that. I told her to come back for a weekend and when I saw her coming off the plane; she looked pale and very thin, washed out looking. She said she was fine, but I figured otherwise, and the break would do her good. I was concerned for her wellbeing, her mental health as well as her physical wellbeing.

The weekend off worked like a treat, she looked fresher and some colour returned to her cheeks, her mood improved, but she was not looking forward to going back to the cauldron. Her letters told me the true story, she felt harassed and intimated by some people on the course, and it was taking its toll on her. I think certain people took advantage of her because of her disarming nature, she was vulnerable to certain types and they took advantage of her. She became distressed about this and became more cautious with people. I was concerned for her; she was under enormous pressure, as she also took on individual tuition with mentally challenged children in order to survive in London.

I wanted to marry Karen after about year or so of the comings and the goings. There was always pressure for time, whether it was in London or back home. There was always a mad last minute panic to drive to Cork airport to board a flight to London. But the little red corvette always came up trumps; in fact, it was a little 1983 ford fiesta, 957 cc, which was nicknamed "The Red Corvette" somewhere along the line. That car was my soul mate too, I loved it with a passion and despite its small engine, it was a giant killer, especially so when it came to the winding country roads. It even had a CD player that came out of a Japanese import, a really cool sound system, though much maligned!

We used to love driving through the Cork and Kerry Mountains in the red corvette, with its retro fitted CD player, playing anything from Willie Nelson to Boxcar Willie, Robert

Cray to Kenny G. Karen loved to travel briskly through the narrow roads with the music turned up nicely. That CD player could have come out of a Nissan skyline with 440 BHP at the wheels! The rate of progress depended on the track being played at that moment.

There was the complicated scenario of the course she was going through and pressure from her mum back home in Canada, who was very demanding of Karen, intellectually and emotionally. She always seemed caught between two stools, and there was I in the middle, making things more complicated.

From the moment we fell in love, I was considered a complication, it was not in the script, it demanded too much of her time and emotions. Meanwhile back home, I was trying to get on with work and make allowances for the many flights to London, in order to look after Karen. I don't think she would have made it through the course without my support, as I wrote to her frequently, giving advice on situations she found extremely distressing, both professionally and privately. I loved being there for her, I thrived in the knowledge I was helping her come through the most difficult time of her life, well, to me it seemed that way.

There was one particular detail that we found very difficult to agree on, that was picking out two wedding rings. We were in Kenmare browsing the shops when we walked in to this little Jewellers shop, De Barra's. We looked at the display cabinets and I said; "That one looks just fine", Karen baulked at the item and beckoned the jeweller out from behind the counter. What followed on from this was pure torment for the next few days. She drew an intricate design on paper of what she wanted and the jeweller said he would have the rings in a fortnight. Later that night, in our hotel, she wondered about modifying the design even more, so the following morning we drove to the jeweller's house to alter the design. The poor man seemed tormented also, but he did manage to manufacture two beautiful wedding bands.

I was always terrified with the thought of giving an after dinner speech at my own wedding. I couldn't put two words together whilst in the spotlight, unless maybe I had a gallon of the devils buttermilk beforehand (Guinness), whereby Dutch courage would have enabled me to rant long into the night, not to mention dancing like Michael Jackson given the appropriate music.

Karen got me to drive down to Glanmore Lake, where we took a walk by the lake and suddenly, she produces the ring and tells me to ask her properly, by going down on one knee. I duly obliged, but something inside told me there was something amiss about it all.

A few weeks later, I knew from her demeanour that she was not entirely happy with the proposal. The "complication" was becoming "overwhelming". We often spoke about having children, but she was dead against it and told me in no uncertain terms we were not to go there. I think that stemmed from her work environment, where she came across so many mentally challenged children and couldn't contemplate having one. Her biological clock was ticking away as was my biological brain; in between was the great wall!

I suppose I pressured her into marrying me at a time when she was an emotional wreck, and vulnerable to a large degree. We had discussed the proposal by phone and hundreds of letters over some months, and she eventually went along with the idea, to the point of going to the church and organising the wedding day and so on. As time went by, I could see from her letters she was becoming increasingly erratic in her thoughts, she became doubtful and distressed, partly due to the intense psychotherapy she was putting herself under on a routine basis and the pressure from me to go ahead with the plan.

She rang me one night at home to tell me she wasn't sure if she was in the right place to get married, she was all over the place emotionally, so after an hour or so on the phone, I told her not to worry, we would shelve all plans for now. Instead, I asked her to look out for a cheap sun holiday for a week, somewhere nice and quiet where we could both switch off and forget about everything that happened. Karen got a deal for a week in that beautiful island of Crete, and we were back on holiday mode again.

I felt a little indifference, disappointment, and relief that we had come through the difficulties together, and would put everything in the back boiler and enjoy the break. It was like we agreed to disagree, and we would forget about it and move on. The week in Crete proved a nice tonic, interspersed with frustration that we would not be getting together, and finality to our relationship. I rented an off road motor bike, a rapid 250 cc four stroke, and proceeded to burn up the roads of Crete with Karen sitting at my back ,loving the warm air gushing over us as we progressed. I was both relieved and distraught, to think that after all the effort of the past year; it would come to nought, impending doom.

Prior to all this drama, we had booked tickets to go to Winnipeg to attend the wedding of a friend of Karen's in August '95, so we kept that appointment. I was looking forward to seeing Canada, but with recent developments, I was a little apprehensive. Karen's state of mind was concerning me, but like everything else in my life, I just went flat out, never considered the negatives, I wanted it so badly. I too felt vulnerable, me being just a humble mechanic, mixing it with all these professional people, feeling intimated by their qualifications, their confidence, their apparently fulfilled lives, their ease of communication, their intellectual abilities.

The wedding was a Mennonite affair, alcohol was frowned upon, how would I survive the day? It was a civil ceremony held in a hotel in Winnipeg. As we sat down to dinner, I befriended a Scottish professor. He lectured in English; I could see that he was dying for a drink, so I asked him if he wanted to come down to the bar in the hotel, and we had a few drinks together. I got on famously with him, the atmosphere at the wedding was fairly subdued by Irish standards, no dancing like a lunatic, falling around the floor, talking shite, getting inebriated. The entertainment was provided by a string quartet, and it was very calm to say the least. This was also a mixed race wedding, and to an outsider like me, I felt a little intimidated by all the high fliers amongst the guests.

Apparently, the groom had gone out of his way to poach Carol along the way. He went for these really ostentatious shows of grandeur, like picking her up one day for a dinner appointment in a stretched Limo, with all the accoutrements. I couldn't believe what I was witnessing; he wasn't Robert Mugabe after all! We joined them for this pre wedding dinner and I felt like the roadrunner, I wanted to turn and run, rapido! I felt like Forrest Gump, but my Mama never said that life was going to be like a box of chocolates!

There were airline pilots, doctors, professors, computer hot shots, geologists and here was I in the middle of them, a humble mechanic, and all I wanted to do was to go outside and pull the cylinder heads off that lovely Shelby Cobra parked outside and lap the valves in for maximum gas flow!

Carol, the bride, was a doctor who worked with aids patients, the groom John, was a computer expert of some sort, very outgoing and suave and seemingly sophisticated. However, Carol spoke to Karen about concerns she had, she said that she didn't seem to have the same passion as we had in her relationship with her fiancée and wondered whether it would get better. It seemed too structured even for her, too managed.

Looking out from the window of the restaurant in late afternoon, I could see the spectacular Prairie sunset, it was magnificent, so colourful. The atmosphere was sedate, people were very courteous and friendly, but I missed the bit of madness that you might get in weddings at home, especially the witty comments. Canadians don't do sarcasm or humour very well, they seemed too correct.. It was an unspoken rule; you never make a derogatory comment about anyone, they were highly sensitive like that.

I was moving in a totally different zone now, and I felt overwhelmed in some ways, but shied away in the background, until it came to doing anything active, like skiing, mountain biking, or climbing. That was my saving grace.

We stayed in the home of another professor in the local university, they were friends of the bride, and I couldn't believe the hospitality they bestowed upon us, never having even met either of us before. They had a beautiful stately house in Winnipeg, and every morning there was a massive table of juices, bacon and eggs, home made croissants, cup cakes, coffee and more. I was seriously impressed.

After breakfast one morning, the conversation turned to books; the professor asked me what I was reading at the time; I froze for a moment, but then told him that I loved reading epic adventure type of books. At that moment, I wanted to burrow my head into any motor magazine nearby to divert attention away from me. The conversation turned to his son suddenly; "Did you read that book last night? I thought it could have been edited better!" I was definitely in deep water.

After the wedding, we got on the bus for our epic tour across Canada, stopping at regular intervals for driver changes and coffee breaks. My favourite town was Banff, and the national park surrounding it. Walk down the street and inevitably you would stumble across Elk and the odd Bear rummaging in a bin. This was real outback territory.

Walking around the town, looking in any direction, there were snow covered peaks jutting up from all angles, stunning knife edge ridges, glacial moraine dropping down into beautiful green lakes and rivers of cool mountain water. I felt at home here, could have stayed for months and months, but we had an agenda and time was hurried. We always seemed to be rushing to get to the next place, and getting on the bus for yet another very long trip was losing its novelty. It was becoming a chore, and I longed to be able to drive all the way down to Vancouver, through the stunning scenery of the Rocky Mountains, which seemed to go on forever.

I loved to hear the very long goods trains coming up through the Rockies with their ghostly fog horn blasts that would echo through the glacial valleys long before they appeared. They seemed to be miles long, endless carriages, it would take them ages to pass.

We visited the Banff Springs Hotel, a sumptuous five star hotel looking out on a stunning vista of Rocky Mountain Splendour, but when we went to the bar, it seemed to be full of Millionaires and modern day gold diggers, pontificating about their incredible fortunes; boring, boring, boring. I would rather have been out with the bears on Mount Assiniboine. Trouble was, you had to do a course on glacial travel and ice climbing techniques before they would let you free on the mountain, more boring, and boring. I need a certificate to go on a mountain! Am I gone mad?

We went rafting down Kicking Horse River one morning, at least you didn't need a certificate for that, I think it was a grade 3 river, a bit tame for my liking, but it was ok, I loved the water gushing over the boat and when we lost a passenger for a brief moment, I laughed my arse off, but was met with astonished looks by the other paddlers.

I loved the Indian names and their connotations with those long forgotten people who tended these same playgrounds with Buffalo and other stock and hunted their merry way throughout this hardened landscape, names like Medicine Hat, Indian Arm, Grousse Mountain, Bear Creek, Moose jaw and many more.

People were so friendly, and interested in where I had come from, wanted to know about the politics and so on, not to mention the IRA and so forth. That same conversation would come up in numerous cities I visited, to the point when I surmised that everyone must have thought Ireland was a country filled with infidels walking around in their bare feet!

After another 16 hour bus trip and we are heading into Vancouver. When we reached the outskirts of the city, I was a little bit apprehensive as the touring was coming to an end. We arrived at Karen's mum's house in North Van, a very tidy and neat home. Her mum was fastidious around the house, everything had to be in the right place, and she was hoovering the white woollen carpet in the living room when we arrived. I was afraid to walk on the lovely carpet as I felt I was being monitored for foreign objects with every step I took. I could see from her mannerisms why Karen was the way she was, meticulous in every detail; nothing left to chance. The relationship between mother and daughter seemed strained, to say the least. They were both too like minded. They were both teachers, highly motivated, very intense.

I went to fill the washing machine and when it was done, I asked Karen did they have a clothes line. Her mum Anne told me that it was forbidden to hang out the clothes in the back garden as there was a golf course out the back and the poor club members might be upset at the sight of hanging laundry, thereby upsetting their golf handicap and any chance of qualifying for the Masters at Augusta!

I was dispatched down to the basement for the night, even though we were lovers for the past couple of years, and I felt like that little boy again, kept out of sight. Karen spent the next few days making contact with her old school district, to see if there were any job prospects at the end of her course. We drove out to meet one of her previous workmates in Maple Ridge, and stayed at her house for a night. Most people seemed to want to relocate outside the city, as property was expensive, and they would move close to their work area.

From my observations of people's lives in Vancouver, I could see that they led very stressful lives, what with the manic commuting to work in the horrendous traffic from 6 am, to the wild partying and extreme outdoor sport activities. Everyone seemed concerned with getting ahead in the world, move to a nicer area, go away as much as possible, preferably skiing to Whistler or sailing on the Sunshine coast on Vancouver Island.

We went to Vancouver Island one weekend with her family and stayed in this lovely log cabin by the sea. We went cycling on some of the fabulous bike trails in the forest and when Karen's bike punctured, I sat her on the bar of my own bike on a downhill section and frightened the life out of her; she hardly spoke to me for the rest of the day.

It was very difficult to find any "craic" chatting to the Canadians, as if they had no sense of humour, took everything too seriously. I walked into it on several occasions by some flippant off the cuff remarks that were met with stony silence and abhorrence in this phonetically correct and so mannerly society. I wilted away from many conversations as I was always socially inept when it came to expressing myself with a captive audience. It would be taken up wrongly as arrogance or ignorance on my part, and I felt an outcast because of that, not suited to this country or its people.

These were really awkward times for me and I would withdraw into myself on numerous occasions, shyness really, which I had since I was a kid and never recovered from, I always tried to avoid those scenarios when I would be found out as vulnerable, reclusive, un-cooperative, and remote. In fact , I was far from that person inside my own mind, I wanted to please people so much and gain approval, it was just that I couldn't express to them in words how I felt.

I had an inferiority complex of sorts, and over the years I've tried to figure out how I came to be in such a state, why was it never figured out at school or the ill fated year spent studying in UCD in the mid 70's, where I would freeze at tutorials when asked to contribute my thoughts on a book or a lecture, and I would blush with shyness and a sweat would run down my back at the thought of being exposed in this way. I was unable to cope with those situations and avoided them at all times.

Perhaps it had something to do with an early childhood accident that I had, when I ran out into the path of an oncoming car when I was 5 years old and suffered a fractured skull. Ever since that accident, I was very conscious of a deep scar in my forehead, which made me feel a bit of a freak for most of my childhood. I was always covering up my forehead, as I thought it was ugly and nasty. I hated getting hair cuts because in those days, inevitably, they cut your hair very short and my scar was exposed for all to see. It was like my brain was exposed. I was ashamed of it, I thought I was different from everyone else, I was incredibly shy, which was the main reason I ran around like a lunatic at any sports activities, but always made sure my fringe was long enough to cover up my disfigurement.

I remember someone took a photograph of me after I came out of hospital with my head shaven and I took one look at it and immediately hid it away from view at the back of the photo album. Years later, I got the picture and tore it up and discarded it, I hated the picture so much.

I was very insecure as a result of this, but I had huge energy levels and burnt myself out running and racing around and getting into devilment. I didn't have the means to articulate my feelings or thoughts at any time, I just brushed it all off with a whimper and an innocent shy smile. But inside, I had hundreds of thoughts going around my head, wasn't sure which ones were appropriate for the moment, thereby my confidence and self esteem grew lower and lower. I would always be the one to be spoken for in the family. Whatever was said, I agreed, just to conform to the status quo. Inside, however, I was eating myself up for not being able to speak out and express my feelings.

I felt like a leper, alienated from conversations, always on the fringes, listening intently, but unable to contribute anything because of my shyness. I felt guilty about that all my childhood life, could find no way through the abyss, felt incompetent as a result, yet when it came to writing down my feelings, I opened up a torrent of passionate emotion, unlimited ability to call things as I saw them in words and descriptive text. I had a passion for writing letters and all my hidden emotions and thoughts emerged from their inner sanctum.

My favourite place in Vancouver was Deep Cove in North Van, it was within a short bus ride of the house, and it had a lovely harbour near the village, with fishing and sail boats bobbing around in the water. I would come down here regularly, rent a bike or a kayak and paddle out around the harbour with its stunning vista, beautiful houses built beside the water with their own little jetties. However, any time I went past them, there seemed to be no signs of life, nobody home, it was eerily quiet. Perhaps they were just trophy houses!

We would often stroll down here together by the water, and one time, a couple of Canada Geese landed only a few feet away. Karen commented that Canada Geese were mated for life, and she wished the same could be said for us, if only. I had my misgivings, as things seemed to be getting increasingly tense between us ever since our trip across Canada.

They seemed to live very stressful lives, from what I gathered, very pressurised living, nobody seemed to have any down time. I did'nt really want to be part of this, and I wondered how I would cope in that scenario. At the time, the likelihood of that happening was remote, but I didn't rule it out. I loved this country, but something told me that it was too structured, too organised and too managed for me. I missed the spontaneity of being able to take off at a moment's notice, as everything had to be planned in advance here. For me, being the impulsive type, that was torture.

However, we were on holidays, and that was the mind set for the moment, and it was great. When it came down to more serious matters, I shied away, non committal, to add to Karen's frustration. I did not want to be tied down, enjoyed my impulsivity, however inappropriate that may have been. I wanted so much to please her and tried to change my manner, but it was not the real me, I felt restrained, confined. I sensed her tensions on numerous occasions, but it always dissipated when we got out in the outdoors. It was only in those awkward social interactions, when it would recur, and that was the pattern for our stay.

She wanted me to read all these self help and personal development books in order to please her; Deepak Chopra's "The Path to Love", Susan Jeffers; "Feel the fear and do it anyway", and so on. I would rather have been reading the life story of Ari Vatanen, or Hugh Macinnes's "Turbochargers," or Lance Armstrong's classic; "it's not about the Bike". I felt like an on-going project at times, work in progress!

It was time to get back to reality with a bang. Boarding the plane to London, I could feel the cold chill in the air, the thought of London after this beautiful vibrant city. How could anyone leave this place? Why would anyone want to leave such a country? Arriving back in Heathrow at an ungodly early hour, we were shepherded into a waiting area, for Immigration documentation checks. As we queued, people were visibly tired and emotional after the long flight, and this last minute process was undignified and draining.

I approached the passport control desk and I was waved through without any delay. As I waited for Karen to come through, there was a delay, a very long delay, and I began to worry when I saw them beckoning someone from the office to have a look at her passport. Her residency visa had elapsed, unknown to her, and she got strict instructions to go to the naturalisation services in South London to reapply for her visa. This involved spending a day queuing and filling out immigration documents. She succeeded in getting the visa and we took a stroll in a park to alleviate the stressful morning.

Things were growing increasingly tense between us now, what with the impending decision Karen had to make regarding her future. She was becoming increasingly erratic in her thoughts, very unsure of herself, about me, whether or not to go back home to Canada, as she had sounded out the work situation on her previous visit. The Art Psychotherapy course had taken its toll, not least because of the intensive psychoanalysis she had to do on herself, week in week out. If you probe yourself that deep on a consistent basis, then I think it leads to self doubts and paranoia to some degree.

I went back home, as I had to go back to work. It was with a sense of relief that I stepped on the plane, and once above the clouds, all anxiety seemed to disappear, gliding through that pristine air above the clouds, bright sunshine, blue skies. I was worried about Karen, I thought she was under tremendous stress, and it was not looking good. I wrote to her a few times that week to try and allay her fears, but from her letters I knew she was anything but calm and coherent.

A few weeks passed and I decided to go over for a weekend, as she did not have the time, due to the intensive nature of her studies. I sensed all was not right this time, as usually, she would meet me at the train station and we would go for coffee. This time, there was no sign of her. I made my way to Peckham to her house, and what met me at the door was a woman in mental turmoil, having a breakdown. I tried to apply some logic to the situation, to calm her nerves, but she was incoherent, made no sense.

We stayed in that night and no progress was made, between phone calls to Canada to her school principle, who demanded to know whether she would turn up for work for the new term, and totally erratic behaviour in between. Neither of us slept for one moment that night, it was a nightmare, and come the morning, I was exhausted from all the mental sparring, she was getting worse by the minute, so I had to leave to catch a flight.

I knew from that moment that things would never be the same between us, she was lost. I knew in my heart that she would go back home, as the pressure from her mum was intense and it seemed inevitable. I had no further contact with Karen, as her mental state deteriorated so much, I figured it was placing more pressure on her. I phoned her mum a week later to find out whether she was safe or not. She had gone back home, and I was relieved she had made it back. Her mum thanked me for looking after her in London.

I tried to get back into my work routine, all alone again, missing the demands of a relationship. Everything seemed so banal, but my conscience was clear, I had done my utmost to please Karen and help her through her course. She passed her final exams, despite the traumas, but she was in a very poor mental state at the end. I could hold my head high in the knowledge that I brought her most of the way, that she would not have made it without my support. I felt really good about that, it was very rewarding.

As the years rolled by, I wondered every day, what would she have been doing at that moment, thought about her constantly. She had laid a new benchmark as regards relationships, as I knew I would never again meet anyone remotely like her. I had no contact with her for years, 5 years to be precise, until one morning in January 99, out of the blue, I got a phone call. It was Karen, asking me how I was. I could hear from her voice that she was back to herself, calm and collected, missing Ireland and the Irish wit and banter.

That time of year, I always longed for a ski trip or mountaineering trip away, so I asked her how snow conditions were out there, and wondered if we could go and play in that magic wonderland again. She mentioned that spring break was coming up and she would have a week off, and she asked me to come over. It didn't take much prompting, as I was itching to go out there to enjoy it, have fun with her again.

I flew from Heathrow one morning a few days later, on a 10 hour flight to Vancouver. I was like a child with anticipation, gleeful with excitement. Flying into Vancouver, the plane flew over this spectacular harbour with snow capped peaks on either side, an absolutely stunning vista. I couldn't wait to get off the plane, to see Karen again, to play in the great outdoors, to laugh with her and joke. Vancouver airport is the most beautiful I've ever seen, has all these lovely sculptures , and a lovely water fall trickling down the centre of the building , wild buffalo and Moose carvings, very authentic. You could feel the pulse of the country in the atmosphere created there.

As I made my way to arrivals, my heart beat a little faster, in the knowledge that I was to be united again with this beautiful woman, it was as good as it gets. When I met her after 5 lonely years, I was smitten by her warmth and genuine affection, regard for me. I still loved her, despite what we had gone through. There was warmth in the air again; the prospect of having fun times again was overwhelming.

Everything seemed to fit like a glove, this woman, this beautiful country, the endless possibilities.

We had a hectic schedule of activities to attend to, there was skiing, mountain biking, sailing in Vancouver harbour, wining and dining with her family and friends, kayak trips in Deep Cove, campervan excursions up the coast, it was a wonderland, and I fell in love again, both with Karen and this awesome country. I was at home, for the first time in 5 years, I was smitten, and I didn't want to leave. I realised that I still loved her, despite our past traumas, and it was with a heavy heart that I departed Vancouver 10 days later.

All the old misgivings were forgotten, we were back on terms and after a few days back home, I picked up the phone and asked her would she marry me. She said yes, and from that moment on, it was all systems go. I applied to the Canadian embassy for a residency visa and work permit, and we agreed to meet again in July, when she would come over to organise all the wedding details. It was all systems go once more; I was like a child in Disneyland, excited beyond belief. I couldn't wait for it to come, I was so eager to get it over and move on with our lives.

I went back to work as usual, time was really dragging, especially after our whirlwind trip. Planning and details were never high on my list, and I found that everything moved excruciatingly slow. The process of applying for the visa was really laboured, as it had to be done in Canada also, and numerous times I got requests for more and more information and documentation from the Embassy. I wanted to get married without all of the paraphernalia, all the fuss, but Karen insisted that it was to be done in almost military style, a gradual assault, culminating in a swift resolution.

The months rolled on and by July I was really looking forward to Karen's visit. She wanted to spend time exploring the countryside, cycling, kayaking, hill walking, going to pub sessions, not to mention organising the wedding mass and reception details. It was a frantic two weeks, we didn't stop to take a breath, such was the pace. She loved West Cork, towns like Union Hall, Castletownshend, Allihies, Kenmare and Killmackillogue in particular. We had the same passions, and she loved the Irish wit, would find endless amusement listening to the conversations of the locals in the small rural pubs. She was intrigued by it all. I loved her company; she was invigorating, totally aware of the idiosyncrasies of the locals, whilst I just laughed it off; "sure we're all mad here"!

Eventually, we picked out two simple gold wedding bands in Tralee and I breathed a sigh of relief. The reception was booked in the Royal Hotel in Killarney, and the wedding ceremony was to be performed in the beautiful Fossa church, just outside Killarney. In addition, we had to go on a pre marital course, which defied logic from my point of view. We had waited long enough and why did we need to gain approval or otherwise from someone unknown to us. The pre marriage course to me was like an accounting exercise, can you afford a home? How much do you make? Do you promise to love and cherish the mortgage? Of course there was a lot more to it, but I didn't want to go there.

I hated any kind of intrusion into our lives; I wanted just to get the whole damned thing over and done with. We had to book flights for her family to Ireland at the end of the millennium, as the wedding day was fixed for December 1999. Her mother being the superstitious type, was worried frantic about the much documented Millennium Bug, and thought the plane would drop out of the sky as a result. I was to organise accommodation in Dublin and Killarney for their stay, and I was to collect them at the airport and drive them to Killarney via the most scenic route. I was a little anxious about all the details.

As time went by, I missed the contact between us, she was so far away, and picking up the phone wasn't the same as meeting face to face. Long distance relationships are tough, and this one was no different. I had too much time to think about things, and that made me uncertain.

Doubts cropped up in my mind, the prospect of not being able to work in Vancouver for the first year perplexed me. I would have to go on a course to update me on work practices over there, and the prospect of having too much time on my hands really bothered me. There is only so much you can do in the great outdoors, and despite all the attractions, I found the bureaucracy stifling. In order to rent snow shoes one day, I had to fill in a form, and when I returned the shoes, I had to fill in another form. The same was true for any activity, they were sticklers for detail. Everything had to be done to the letter of the law, and they all seemed to conform like sheep. I felt under scrutiny from some of her friends, didn't consider myself smart enough, whilst being streetwise. The bureaucracy involved with immigration seemed never ending.

I kept in touch with Karen by phone for the remaining months; the two weeks together had passed in a flash. Every detail of the wedding was planned, right down to the seating arrangements, the wine, and the toast after dinner. The readings for the wedding mass were picked out as were the numerous other details. When it came to sending out invitation, it got very complicated. Karen wanted to design them and hand write them individually, with emblems of the Canadian Maple Leaf and our own Tri colour. Being an artist, she wanted show her creative style. What irritated me most was when she included photos of both of us in various stages of our lives, with the inclusion of one particularly nauseating one of me as I may appear when old and decrepit, a mock up if you like. This brought images back to me of that famous photo taken after my childhood accident and the humiliation it bestowed upon me. I stayed quiet, went along with it.

My other gripe was when she wanted me to sign a pre-nuptial agreement, stating that I had no property rights whatsoever if the marriage didn't last. To make matters even more complicated, her mother offered to cash in her pension in order to buy a house for Karen. I duly signed the legal document, which effectively meant that I would be absolutely flat broke with no rights to property or investments of any kind. This hinted to me as a lack of trust and faith in our ability to move forward as a couple, and it frustrated me.

Summer passed quickly into autumn, and I was getting increasingly doubtful about Emigrating to Canada. I would miss racing up the Reeks on a Sunday morning, running back to the car in time for the throw in Croke Park for the big GAA matches, the rolling commentary of Micheal o Muirheartaigh;

"Pat Fox out to the 40 and grabs the sliothar, I bought a dog from his father last week. Fox turns and sprints for goal, the dog ran a good race last Tuesday in Limerick, Fox to the 21, fires a shot, it goes to the left and wide.........and the dog lost as well".

Not to mention bleating of lambs on the mountain, the freedom of it all, going back to Kate Kearny's for a pint or two, the banter of the pony men in the gap, the madness of it.

Everything was set up to go by October; my stag night was to be held in November in Knocknagree. Towards the end of October, facing Halloween, it began to get frantic. Everyone seemed to be on a high, in anticipation of the impending nuptials and the prospect of having a new holiday destination to visit. I decided on the Thursday of the Bank holiday weekend, to travel over to Vancouver, as I was increasingly unsettled about the move. There was the additional matter of looking for a house in Vancouver, somewhere nice we could settle into. Karen was very surprised when I told her of my visit, as money was tight and we had to be careful and budget for the wedding and all the travel surrounding it.

I flew to Vancouver for Halloween, and in the seat beside me was a Pakistani man. We talked about Canada and he told me about his business there, which involved clothing manufacture and I asked him about marriage and told him about my predicament. He did not give me any advice, but I wanted him to tell me not to do it, I felt so uncertain about the prospect. Arriving in Vancouver airport, I was met by a seemingly nervous Karen; she seemed distant, in contemplative mood, disturbing me somewhat. All of a sudden, things seemed to get too serious, I sensed a change in attitude, a worry. Even getting out of the carpark was fraught with difficulties, it was wet and cold, and the atmosphere was tense. I felt uncomfortable, wary, like a man facing the guillotine.

We drove on to her house, and everything seemed strange, the fun seemed to have gone, the serious business was at hand and it was showing. We went to her brother's house on Halloween night and went around the neighbourhood with their kids trick or treating. I couldn't believe how enthusiastically the Canadians took to Halloween; they made a huge effort to decorate their homes with all the paraphernalia and spooky costumes. When we got back to the house, the conversation seemed very serious; I felt like that little boy again, nothing to contribute, out in the cold, withdrawn. I could see from the reaction in the house that they sensed all was not well, they looked concerned.

The following morning we had an appointment with an estate agent, to show us some properties nearby. Some of the houses were totally inappropriate, huge rambling houses with too many rooms for just a couple of people. One house in particular, was like a custom Halloween house. It was tilted to one side, as the foundation was sinking, and when I walked around a bedroom upstairs, I had to stop myself running forward towards a window, as there was a steep decline in the floor. Another house in Deep Cove was absolutely stunning, it had a stream of mountain water running through the back garden, and it was meticulous in every detail, had stunning views of the harbour out front.

We had to call to a graphic designer in order to change little details in the hand written invitations. Being a total perfectionist, Karen was never happy with the finished article, there was always a better way, her attention to detail was mind boggling, very fussy. I would have gone along with anything, to get it over with. We took a stroll along the pier near Deep Cove and I could see Karen's mood was sombre.

Karen spoke about her father's illness and his final days in hospital. He died of a brain tumour and he had reverted back into a child like state in those last few days. She mentioned her concerns about my medical history and wondered whether I could have ended up the same way. She also mentioned that she didn't want to be my psychotherapist, yet she insisted that once married, we should have weekly meetings to discuss our progress. Now that totally freaked me out.

She took out a joint and smoked it. I laughed it off, why all the worry and concern? I would have been happy just going to the little church in Las Vegas, where drive through weddings were the norm, why torture oneself with all these details? I was more uncertain than ever on this trip and she saw that I wasn't happy. I told her that there was no way I could I meet her exacting standards, that I wasn't good enough for her, I was unworthy. I was unable to compete with her, on her own terms, so I went into limp home mode. The engine management light came on in the dashboard.

I was in trouble, and I had taken on too much intensity and scrutiny. I wanted to run, run, and run. My diagnostic system was in failure, in terminal decline. I couldn't possibly live up to her expectations, even though I loved her with a passion. She asked me what was the problem, and I could not put it into words, I was now in survival mode, trying to hide my disappointment and unable to articulate my thoughts, though inside, I knew I could not be the person she wanted.

She had often spoken to me of the need to change myself to meet Canadian standards. I knew in my heart and soul, there was no way that was going to happen, so I bluffed through the remaining days, despite her insistence on me staying longer to discuss our problems. It was with relief that she drove me to the airport, balling crying all the way, inside in the terminal building as well, whilst at the check in desk. I felt terrible, I had betrayed her, but the truth was, I couldn't go through with it; I would be deceiving her and fooling myself.

It was the loneliest and saddest flight I had ever taken. I had to face going back home with my news and to cancel all the wedding arrangements. It broke my heart to do so, it had taken so long to get so far, yet in a couple of hours, I was dismantling my future destiny. I went through my room and tore up about 300 letters I had received from her over the previous year, discarded any photographic memories of her, and I tried to blank all the images out of my life. It was very traumatic for me, and I struggled to get back into a routine.

My stag night was due to be held the weekend after I came back from Canada, but I went ahead with it anyhow, it was an excuse to get pissed and party the night away, all bets were off. The night went down like a treat, everyone else was having a ball, but I was crying my heart out inside. I tried to make excuses for my actions, but I had none, I just fobbed it off as just a bad experience.

For years afterwards, I considered going over to Vancouver to try and meet with Karen and talk about the reasons why I withdrew from the marriage. It irked me so much and I could never find a solution, she wouldn't talk to me, her mum wouldn't let me talk to her on the few occasions I got connected. It was heartbreaking for me because I couldn't articulate my thoughts to the people that mattered. At home, things just carried on as if nothing happened, but nothing could be further from the truth, I was eaten up inside with guilt and torment.

Chapter 3

LIFE AFTER KAREN

Not a day went by without thinking about what had happened. I was in shock, it was worse than death, and I thought about her constantly, what would she be doing now? How would she cope? It was never ending. I tormented myself, lambasted myself for not having the guts to go through with it. I don't know how I survived Christmas that year.

I heard on the grapevine, that a few friends were going to Morocco on a cheap holiday, bringing their bikes along. I jumped at the opportunity, to banish the blues. I was back at the start line again, back to go, and got out of jail. Getting on the tarmac at Agadir airport, I kissed the ground, relieved to be free again, relishing the thought of mountain biking in the heat of North Africa. We had a small apartment in the city which we used as a base, and once we assembled the bikes, we made our way to the local taxi rank to haggle about the best price for a trip into the anti-atlas mountain region.

Four of us, including bikes and back packs, squeezed into an old Mercedes, like sardines in a tin, bike bits strapped on to the roof, for our long drive to Tafraoute, which was going to be our base for a few nights. The driver had to get permission from the police to leave the city, and he had to attend to the small matter of repairing an indicator lamp, which was broken and didn't work. This entailed driving around a shanty town on the outskirts of Agadir, looking for a mechanic to repair the said item. Talk about ingenuity, we pulled up outside this seemingly derelict little shop and the engineer appeared and had a look at the lamp. He proceeded to get a plastic bottle, orange in colour, and cut a lens shaped like the lamp, and wired it on to the lamp.

We were on our way across very hot and arid countryside, and when the driver would pass Muslim women by the roadside, he would honk his horn and wave his arms in an animated display of passion. Apparently, it was his first time driving out this part of the country and we had to navigate for him as he had no map or sense of direction, no sat nav for this boy!

It was fascinating to see his reactions to this new terrain; he was like a child on a new adventure. The Moroccan people were very noble, you agreed a price after seemingly hours of haggling, but they got on with it afterwards, regardless, no quibbling. We arrived in Tafraoute a few hours later, in the middle of the Anti Atlas Mountains, and after we unloaded our stuff, the driver shook our hands in a refreshing display of gratitude, happy to meet, sorry to part. The people were so humble over there; it was an eye opener for me, in comparison to the ravenous nature of life back home, the pre-Celtic Tiger era.

We were in this bar near Tafraoute one evening when a number of tribal Tuareg people arrived in the door with their map and compass, having walked from God only knows where in the desert, dressed in full tribal robes, it was really exotic. It hit home to me how simple life could be lived, without all the paraphernalia of the Western world. These people spoke fluent French and English as well as their own native dialect. The Berber people were beautiful souls; they seemed to live in another world to ours.

It reminded me of days walking in the wilderness back in the Kerry hills, with my map and compass, only for the fog to descend suddenly and I had no bearings to go on. Sometimes I walked for hours on end only to end up back at a very familiar spot, the point where I first got lost, and I had to descend in order to find a bearing on my map and to get back to my starting point. I had done that numerous times over the years, but there was something soulful about it.

It was invigorating to witness life in Morocco, totally at odds to what we were used to at home. I always wanted to escape the madness of Christmas, all the superfluous spending and drinking. In the back of my mind, I was constantly thinking of Karen, had I made a massive mistake? I couldn't escape from the thought; it would haunt me for the foreseeable future.

I tried to phone Karen, but her mum answered the phone. She said it would be better if she didn't talk with me. I was gutted, and choked for words. I tried numerous times to ring, but dropped the phone when it dialled out. This would happen on numerous occasions, and I always choked at the vital moment. I would try and go back to my routine, but it was eating me up, I knew I couldn't contemplate meeting anyone remotely like Karen ever again, I had lost a golden opportunity, everything else would be bullshit in comparison. I had made my bed, and now I had to lie in it.

From this moment on, I was back to my old hated self, that lad that was stuck in the corner at home with his Mammy depending on him now even more than ever before. I was unable to move forward, to develop as I had wished to with Karen by my side, but that was now thrown to the wolves, I was in terminal decline mentally with no prospect of meeting anyone remotely like Karen ever.

This would be the pattern of my life for the foreseeable future, I was on auto pilot. If not for my outdoor regime of activities, I would have succumbed long ago to some dreadful condition. The mountain was my saviour, getting out in all conditions, no matter how wild, I thrived in them. No gully was steep enough or slippery enough for me to attack, especially when I was on my own. I was intoxicated more so than ever, it was my only outlet from the pain in my heart and soul. I would push myself beyond the pain barrier on numerous occasions during the following years.

One Sunday in November of '04, I was running down "The Bone" in the Reeks, where the ground was very soft. As I ran down the boggy descent, I overextended my right leg whilst running at full pelt, and I heard a painful jolt in my knee. I had torn a cruciate ligament, and slowed down the pace a little, but as I had a lot of ground to cover, I kept going, only to fall into the river Gaddagh when crossing it. I suppose it kept the swelling down, but I made it back to the car and I had to lift my right leg into the car in order to drive home. I went for a pint first; my knee was getting bigger by the sip, until I could barely walk out to the car.

I was gutted by this injury, as I had booked a trip with Killarney Mountaineering club to Ecuador in South America, departing in January 05, where we were going to climb the highest active volcano in that country, Cotopaxi. I knew my chances of recovering by that time were remote. I was also self employed, which meant taking time off work, and I didn't need that. I had an MRI scan on my knee in December 04, and the consultant advised me to forget about the trip, it may require further surgery or lots of rehabilitation in order to get back the muscle tone. I was gutted. I was on crutches for 10 days, and I tried to walk unaided once the swelling went down, very gingerly. There was going to be a long road to recovery, to get back to my previous fitness level.

I got a grain of hope when the consultant told me I could possibly avoid surgery if I built up the quad muscles, make them stronger. That was all I needed to hear, and by Christmas I said I would go for a walk up the hag's glen, the route on to Carrauntuohill. Conditions were icy with lots of snow, and as I walked, I felt better by the minute, eventually going to the summit, with no gear whatsoever. My hands were numb with the cold and I borrowed a pair of gloves on the summit, I was ecstatic, the trip was back on as far as I was concerned. I said to myself that I could walk up to the huts and stay the night there and return the same way in the morning.

As it turned out, the rest had done me good and I felt strong and able to continue with the group on most of the planned routes. It involved getting acclimatised to the altitude for the first few days, then gradually climbing smaller volcanoes of 3000 metres or so, before attacking Cotopaxi some days later. It was a stunningly beautiful mountain, and from our refuge, we could look through a telescope and follow the progress of people up near the summit, including one party of Americans who skied down from the summit. Visibility was very clear early in the morning, bright sunshine, blue skies, very cold.

South America for me was the complete anti dote to life in Ireland. The pace of life was so slow, if you wanted anything done, it would always be "Mañana", no pressure; time stood still, no one rushed around tripping over themselves. This was the start of the Celtic Tiger madness that would engulf Ireland, and I wondered to myself, what was it all about? These South Americans had it down to a tee. On numerous occasions I came across people asleep in a ditch, I figured they must be dead or drunk, but no, it was siesta time.

I loved getting on the Pan American highway for a new adventure, every day brought new territory, new experiences, different people, and it was really stimulating. Everyone seemed so friendly and eager to please you. On numerous occasions we would come across small pick up trucks with the whole family sitting in the back smiling and waving at us in our bus, they seemed so happy and cheerful.

Passing through the town of Ambato, I couldn't but be impressed with all the garages and car accessory shops offering everything from a dodge V10 engine to alloy wheels for a miserly

Suzuki Swift. It was Motown as far as I was concerned, a boy racers dream, with VW beetles fitted with V8 Chevy engines and Honda Civics with similar make up. Insurance was an optional extra here, if you had an accident, it was up to both drivers to settle with each other for the damage, outrageous as that may seem.

This was my second trip to South America. I had previously visited Chile in late 2001, just after the Twin Towers atrocities, we flew American Airlines to JFK in a very subdued and quiet cabin. It was eerily quiet, and the plane had rows and rows of empty seats. Arriving in Santiago a day later, it couldn't have been more different to the chaos at JFK airport, everything moved down a couple of gears, it was hot and sultry. We had to adjust our mindset accordingly, to blend in with the pace. People in this part of the world seemed more soulful, content with their lot, enjoyed life despite being very poor. I envied them, what were we doing wrong? I didn't want to leave here, it suited my temperament, my outdoor lifestyle, I could have been a Gaucho.

We brought our bikes with us to Chile, and three of us spent the two weeks climbing active Volcanoes like Villarica, Osorno, and a few epic nights wild camping in various national parks. Two of the bikes were stolen from the back of our van in Temuco, and we ended up for most of the afternoon trying to explain what the bikes looked like. We scribbled down bike frames with the manufacturer's names and their colour, but really I think the police were having a laugh at us, there wasn't a hope in hell of getting the bikes back.

We had intended to drive down all the way to Patagonia, but underestimated the huge distances involved. We got as far as the border of Chile-Argentina when the customs men wouldn't let us through as we didn't have documentation from the hire company to drive into Argentina. As we slept rough the previous night, we looked like Farc terrorists from Columbia and the customs people were suspicious about our plans. But we did get to Chiloe, that famous island where Charles Darwin expounded on Evolution of the Species. I was evolving at a rapid rate out here!

I loved climbing those volcanoes, as most of them were around the 3000 metre mark and one didn't need a huge amount of technical equipment to climb them. They were also very quiet, no lines of people as in the Alps, total freedom. The motto in South America seemed to be; "live for today, for tomorrow you may die", it was great.

I had to get back home and face the drudgery, the mind numbing pain in my heart, the seemingly insatiable greed of some individuals, and here was I trying to carve out some kind of living for myself. The trip to Chile hit home to me how life could be lived very modestly and at the same time happily. My mum would have loved it out here, you could hang the clothes out and they would be dry in one hour flat! No smash and grab between the showers!

When I came home in 2002, the currency had changed to the ill fated Euro, and there were tail backs of people out in the streets, queuing to change their old notes for the new currency. It was like the gold rush in Klondike all over again. It beggared belief. I wanted to run away from all of this madness.

But I was stuck at home now, my poor mum was depending on me to a large extent, her health was failing. I felt stifled at home, no means of expression in any form, hence my excursions into the mountains or on a bike. They were my relief valve, just like a waste gate in a turbo, when the pressure gets too high; the waste gate opens to stop the engine from detonating. My waste gate was working overtime on a daily basis, what with the demands at home and work, as well as my emotional pain.

I used to love spending quiet time with Karen. We would go to some quiet hotel and chat and spend hours talking about every subject under the sun, they were really tender moments together. I was very interested in art psychotherapy and the inter action involved. It amazed me to see the amount of preparation she would go through for a class and the self analysis she would put herself through. Any time she handed in a thesis, she would ask me to read it and ask me for my opinion. It was no wonder, in hindsight, that she eventually cracked under the pressure.

I saw friends getting married, getting on with their lives, family members too, and I felt like a reject, unwanted, unloved. How could I recover from this trauma?

I did meet another woman later on, and I did love her, but she had two kids to look after and I felt like I was superfluous to her needs, eventually getting so frustrated that I was driving to her house one night on Christmas Eve and I turned the red corvette upside down and slid on the roof for some distance, getting out the front windscreen after kicking it out. I had no injuries apart from a gashed forehead and bruised spine. It had a parallel with those huge Nascar crashes but with no spectators apart from a few startled rabbits! And there was no applause from the crowd as I made my escape from the wreckage.

Of course I had drink taken, and I was driving like a man possessed, but I was possessed, with anger, torment and rage. I had an identical accident 25 years previously when I rolled my beetle into a stream. I was driving to Tralee one cold and icy morning, when I rounded a bend at speed and I slid down the road for 500 metres before turning upside down in a field. As the car was lying upside down in the water, I listened Bob Marley playing "oh what a rat race," it was the same scenario in this latest crash, I was in the middle of the rat race, very unhappy with my life, but no Bob Marley.

I got back home after the accident, quietly slipped in the door to bed, blood on my pillow, unable to sit for 3 days. I tried to hide my predicament for as long as possible, as I didn't want to upset my poor mother, but the following morning all was revealed, well, not everything, I was always very good at concealing my adventures, just carried on as if nothing happened.

Planning was never high on my agenda, I lived in the moment. I often wondered what was all the rushing about for, nobody seemed to have time to stop and chat. People were getting obsessed about climbing the property ladder, having a 4 by 4 jeep and flying off to the sun as much as possible, acquiring stuff. You couldn't avoid the mania that went on.

I celebrated a milestone birthday in '06, my 50th year on this planet. I had to organise this in perfect detail. My buddy, Chuck, who had poured concrete in the skyscrapers of Manhattan in the eighties, had come home and opened a lovely restaurant in Killarney. I organised a party there for 50 people or so and booked a couple of cool musicians, Hank Wedell and Ray Barron, to play after dinner. Hank was a singer song writer, he could have been a Rhinestone Cowboy such was his dress code and demeanour, whilst Ray was the master of the Mandolin, and he made that mandolin work really hard for its keep, he played mountain music that would have done credit to the founding father of Bluegrass ; the great Bill Munroe!

It turned out to be the one of the most memorable nights of my life, people were out dancing in droves, and people came in off the street when they heard the brilliant music, whilst "cheers and thanks man" provided us with trays upon trays of pints of Guinness from his hostelry nearby. Someone produced a cake in the shape of my little red corvette with number plates and all. It was a fitting end to half a century of life on the fringes.

On my 50th year, I entered the Killarney Adventure Race at the last minute. I had looked at the proposed route and thought that it was ideally suited to me. But in order to enter the event, you had to raise a lot of money, and there was no way I could raise the funds. So I asked the organiser, Con Moriarty, if anyone needed a last minute replacement due to injury or else, I would fill in for them.

On the eve of the event, I got a phone call from Con asking whether I was serious about it; Of course I was serious, would a Christian Brother refuse a drink? And so I lined up at the start near the tunnel on the Kenmare road with my team mate Paddy.

The race started with a paddle up the Long Range to Lord Brandon's cottage, and from there a run of 10k up to the Bridia Valley. From there, it was a mountain run from Curraghmore Lake to the top of the Hags Tooth, then an abseil down from the Hag and on to the Hags Glen, from there , cycling out the Hags Glen and up over Strickeen mountain and down into the Gap of Dunloe and on to the finish at Dunloe golf club. I can honestly say it was the best event ever; I loved every inch of the adventure and finished in a respectable time. I felt so good at the finish that I could have done it in reverse after a brief respite and a pint of Guinness!

In reality, I was happy just being able to pay the bills, and then I would head off to the mountains or on the bike for almost every weekend. I was just as happy with a new pair of mountaineering boots. Everyone seemed to be so stressed out, never seemed happy with their lot, always looking for the unattainable. I tried to follow along, knowing in my heart and soul that I had left a gilded opportunity go, and I regretted it daily. Being overly conscientious, I would criticise myself regularly, my work, my performance on the mountain or on the bike, you'd swear my life depended on it.

My brother's health was ailing at this time, he had suffered chronic rheumatoid arthritis since he was a young man, and he would come home to my mums regularly for lunch and he would go to bed for a couple of hours afterwards, before returning to work. It was tough to witness his suffering on a daily basis; it had a profound affect on me and my mum. Things would get worse in the years to follow, as he suffered kidney failure as a result of the medication administered to him over the years. He went on to have a kidney transplant, successfully, but eventually he succumbed in the autumn of '07. This was a crushing blow for my mum. She had looked after him for years on end; she was after all, a carer for most of her life, what with my dad suffering from Parkinson's disease for 20 odd years. It took a heavy toll on my mum, emotionally and physically.

It was very difficult to come to terms with all this agony. I tried to get back into my regular routine, but found it very tough. Work was getting scarcer, I was expected to do more at home, and on top of that, I had a depressant bully to deal with at work. Over the years, I would ask this guy, The Grim Reaper, to come and help me with diagnostic testing on cars. Not a day would go by without him assassinating my character, or that of a customer of mine.

I still can't figure out to this day why I allowed it to happen. I was always under fierce pressure at work when he would arrive, and it would begin almost immediately. I hadn't the time to stop and think about it, there was a job to be done and I had to get the car fixed. I would always breathe a sigh of relief when he left the premises. My self confidence was low enough at the time, but he drove it further into the ground and I ignored it to my peril. He destroyed my self esteem, criticised my friends, and destroyed any ambitions I may have had, no matter how small they may have been.

During the run up to my impending wedding plans with Karen, he bad mouthed even her. I knew that this was intolerant, but I kept my mouth shut, even though my anxiety was increasing daily with the prospect of emigrating again. Bullies are covert, are masters of manipulation and conceit. This was the last straw for me, not alone was I berating myself, but I had someone who was more than willing to kick me into the ground on a regular basis, yet I still gave him plenty of work, but he always threw it back on my face with a sly ugly comment . He continually undermined my work, my workshop practices, my friends, everything really.

My self esteem was on a totally downwards spiral, I felt incompetent, useless, and unable to come to terms with myself, I was full of guilt and remorse. I didn't need to be sabotaged as well. I carried on as best I could, though I was paralysed inside, unable to find a way out. I saw friends getting married, moving on with their lives, seemingly happy, yet I was stuck in a rut, having falling down a crevasse, with no way out.

One morning in May 05, I was using a slide hammer to remove a wheel bearing from a car, and when I gave it a few tugs, it wouldn't budge. I stepped away from it for a while, had a rethink, before attacking it with such venom that I failed to notice that the rage inside me, the years of frustration and torment, the failed relationship, got me into such a state that I injured both my wrists as a result.

Six weeks later, my wrists got very sore, and of course, I just shrugged it off as another difficult job; it would heal itself in time.

I worked on for the next few years, my wrists getting increasingly painful and weak. I visited consultants, got cortisone injections numerous times, had laser treatment a few times, all to no avail. When I discovered that I could no longer do the same jobs with the same intensity, I got worried, very concerned. This was my life; it was all I could do. By the autumn of 08, the pain got so severe that I went to a rheumatologist, and I had numerous scans, bone scans, wrist scans, MRI scans. Eventually I went back to the consultant to be told that I had Rheumatoid Arthritis.

It was like a death sentence for me. I was devastated, and on the drive back from Cork, my mind was working overtime. I could picture myself in a wheelchair or with walking sticks, disabled, horror of horrors. Having seen first hand what it could do to ones body from my brother's experience, I could see no way back for me, it was death and destruction.

Chapter 4

Meltdown

I figured my life was over; I had nothing left to give, no way forward. I spiralled into a severe depression, became suicidal. Christmas 08 was a nightmare. I was curled up in bed for 6 weeks without sleeping. My hands and wrists were in ferocious pain, along with the emotional turmoil on top of it. I got up in the middle of the night and went for a walk, but really all I wanted to do was end it all.

I would go for walks in places that I had frequented over years and years of hill walking, and considered jumping off a cliff or a bridge, considered the implications, massive spinal or head injuries, ending up a quadriplegic or otherwise? How would my family cope? When I realised I could no longer work, it really hit me like a sledge hammer. I went over every single episode in my life when I did something crazy or too adventurous, and tortured myself for being such a fool. I got totally paranoid as a result. I couldn't face going to the shops, going to town, going for a drink.

I had seen over the previous years, how some people I had barely known, had committed suicide, and I always wondered how they could be driven to such extremes, such violence, and such termination. I remembered in particular, their vacant stares, seemingly tortured souls, exposed for everyone to see, but nobody seemed to take notice, they avoided contact, frightened to be associated with such toxicity. It was frightening to see that expression in their faces, yet here was I, in the same place, gutted with guilt, in extraordinary pain, emotionally and physically.

I didn't want to eat, didn't want to wash; I hated myself for bringing so much torment upon myself and others around me. I kept avoiding being caught in any kind of social gathering; I was comatose with grief, unable to function. I hid in my bedroom or took a walk in very remote places at all hours of the morning, having walked waist high into rivers, inhaled camping gas fumes, considering the various ways to end the pain. I considered myself sub human, unworthy to be in this world. I wanted to starve myself, anything to get me out of the torment.

I went firstly to a counsellor, but self affirmation therapy to me at that stage was like trying to stop the Titanic sinking with a lifebuoy. She suggested art therapy, Jesus Christ, hadn't I gone through all that with Karen, and little did I know, the wheel had turned full circle. I was beyond redemption of any kind; the counselling was of no help.

An appointment was then made with a Psychologist. I made my way down for the appointment and the first thing she said to me was that it would cost me 120 Euros for the first session and only 90 for subsequent visits. Here was I, my business gone, suicidal, having to cough up the few meagre Euros I had left to lift me out of a seemingly black hole. That didn't help. She prescribed anti depressants, and I was wary of any medication, never mind anti depressants. She said they would take around 6 weeks to kick in. Every second was ticking away in my mind, 6 weeks seemed interminably long.

I took the anti depressants, but in my mind, I thought they would make no difference. I fought them all the way, refused to admit to myself that I needed help. The torture went on over Christmas, eventually resulting in me being admitted to the psychiatric ward in Tralee General Hospital. It was a voluntary admission, as I was unable to function, didn't want to go on, I was scared and frightened. The stigma of being admitted to the unit was very difficult to ignore. I felt unworthy, dirty.

I was relieved in a way, being admitted to hospital. What faced me was worse than anything I have ever encountered in my life, totally degrading. I was self diagnosing, of course, and it was all extreme and negative. I had googled every mental illness before my incarceration in Tralee, and of course that multiplied my trauma a thousand fold!

In my own mind, I considered myself insane, beyond help, and medication therapy, which is what it really was, seemed totally inept to me. I needed someone to hold my hand, to tell me that it would be all right, that I would come out of this intact. What followed were short meetings with psychiatrists and psychologists who were taking notes constantly, trying to find the best drug therapy for me.

I came across lost souls in there, schizophrenics, manic depressives, alcoholics, broken people of all persuasions. I figured I must have been worse than any of them, as some of them just sat in front of a huge wide screen TV, rocking their heads forwards and back, making incoherent sounds and they had a horrifying vacant stare in their eyes. The nurses seemed to be dispensing chemists as far as I could see, awaiting any sudden violent psychotic outburst in the room. The tension in the air was palpable.

I just wanted to lie in bed, read a book or a magazine, to take my mind away from the truth. I came across a book cupboard and delved through anything and everything I could read. Most people sat in front of the TV all day, watching degrading programmes like Jeremy Kyle, or some other like minded drivel. Arguments occurred like spontaneous combustion, when it came to changing channels. There was music playing deafeningly loud in the other end of the room, and as I tried to turn it down, I was met with very aggressive language and imminent threats of violence.

There was a lovely photograph on the wall of the gap of dunloe, a much loved place close to my heart. I had descended from the head of the gap countless times on my mountain bike at breakneck speed; it was my own cresta run, like the famous downhill ski run in Switzerland. Each time I would descend, I would try and cut the corners as sharp as I could, in order to maintain my speed going forward, numerous times I came too close to the wall on my descent, but without falling. I patted myself on the back afterwards, saying to myself; "you must get the perfect line next time". I told myself that I would never again be able to do such a feat, my life was over as any kind of athlete, I had squandered any opportunities that came my way.

When asked by a psychiatric nurse whether I had OCD, I brushed it off in self defence. Of course I had, I remember numerous times after rebuilding the front of an engine, I would re- check that everything was done exactly as it said in the manual, and then I would check it again. It was with baited breath that I would turn the ignition key after doing a particularly difficult job, only for all the tension to disappear when it fired up, music to my ears, I could relax and just polish it off slowly. I got such satisfaction from hearing that engine running as smoothly as a mouse's heart.

If it was a particularly powerful machine, I would leave the engine to warm up for 20 minutes or so before departing on an adrenaline run out the nearest quiet road. This was ecstasy for me; this was my drug, anything that would fuel adrenaline. Any misconceptions I had were blown out the exhaust in a cacophony of sound.

Team meetings were an absolute nightmare for me. I always dreaded being in a scenario where I was under intense scrutiny, and especially in a small room no bigger than a garden shed, where there were 6 or 7 people sitting taking notes constantly, ticking off boxes, scrutinising every response I had. It brought me back to my history class when we were studying the Spanish

Inquisition of the 15th century. I felt I was in a torture chamber, on a rack, they were winding the rack, trying to get a response from me, but nothing was forthcoming. I just nodded in agreement to whatever was suggested at the particular moment, in fact, anything to get out of there, to go back and watch that depressing Jeremy Kyle show or whatever was on screen at the time.

Before these meetings, I was given a sheet of paper the day before, with a few questions determining my progress, on a scale of 1 to 10. What did I learn from last week? How did I intend to move forward? Did I still feel suicidal? I couldn't even decide what my thoughts were for a second, never mind the following week. My favourite question was; what are your current thoughts? Any current thoughts were firstly, to avert any current thoughts out of my mind, in order to dodge the question and get the fuck away from the inquisition, get back out into the mess and eat a packet of those horrible gooey biscuits and down a gallon of coffee, and berate myself yet again for getting in to this mess. What an idiot!

Bed was my sanctuary, except for the fact that I was sharing the room with 6 or sometimes 7 other people, with one smelly toilet nearby. Most people would sleep, of course they would, they were drugged up to the eye balls, and they didn't want to wake from this nightmare. Sometimes, late at night or early mornings, some poor devil would be dragged into the ward kicking and screaming, ranting and raving, frothing at the mouth, head exploding with expletives. It would take a number of Gardai and several nurses to calm them, until they would be sedated eventually with a rapidly infused cocktail of drugs. It was very disturbing to witness; my heart was pounding with anxiety at the thought of it.

One particular morning, I went to the toilet only to witness the abhorrent sight of bits of excrement all over the floor. It stayed like that for days, and when I complained to a nurse, he said; "that's the way it is, put up with it". I was devastated. Were we not entitled to basic hygiene levels? Animals wouldn't live in that filth, not to mention the possibility of contacting numerous infections, and the smell was horrendous.

No one batted an eye lid at the nurses desk, this was the norm for us low life's; we were beneath normal realms of compassion, of human worth. I dreaded walking around in my slippers, as god only knows what I was carrying around, not to mention the smell. This episode really hit home to me the status quo. I was in here for no good reason, it wasn't supposed to be a hotel, but they could at least have made the basics somewhat hygienic.

The hours dragged on, the mindlessly boring routine, the fresh air walks in the morning, where a nurse would accompany us like sheep, out around the hospital grounds to the shop. There would be a small gathering in the morning when a newspaper would have been produced and a nurse proceeded to read out the headlines. I could have written the bleedin headlines in a whimper for god's sake, yet here I was, supposed to look interested in all the crap news stories of the time, the property bust, the suicides of developers, the dreadful weather, the banking crisis.

The nurses administered the medication in the mornings, or the chemical brothers, as I called them in my own mind. At the team meetings, if your mood did not pick up, the dosage would be upped substantially, in the hope that your mood would improve. I dreaded the prospect of more and more medication being administered to me, how could my mood improve inside here?

I would have preferred to be in mountjoy prison, where I would surely be treated better. I looked out the window to see the snow covered mountains , Caherconree and other hills that I would have run up and down countless times, whilst tormenting myself for not keeping my head, and missing out on all the club walks at the time. It seemed a million miles away from where I stood. Of course, I would never, ever, be able to run up and down the mountains again, getting back to the car in a lather of sweat, looking forward to listening to the outstanding commentary of Micheal o Muircheartaigh;

"And Brian Dooher is down injured. And while he is, I'll tell ye a little story. I was in Times Square in New York last week, and I was missing the championship back home". So I approached a news stand and I said; "I suppose ye wouldn't have the Kerryman, would ye"? To which the Egyptian behind the counter turned to me and he said; "Do you want the North Kerry edition or the South Kerry edition?" He had both. So I bought both. "And Dooher is back on his feet".

I didn't want to leave this cesspit. I was fed and watered, and the longer I stayed, the less chance I had of getting back to reality. I was stuck in time, couldn't face the outdoor world. I was getting institutionalised, became numb and cold, unable to talk with any measure of coherence. I didn't want any visitors. Eventually I wandered out on my own, to take a stroll into town, had a coffee and even went for a pint. I was so ashamed to meet anyone as I didn't want them to know where I was. I sat on my own, usually in a corner, read whatever paper I could lay my hands on, it was so lonely. I may as well have been from Mars; such was my self imposed exile.

It was nice to stroll out in the fresh air, but if there was any delay on my part, I would get a phone call from the nurse, enquiring about my whereabouts. I felt like a criminal, all I was missing was a micro chip implanted in me. There was no room for impulsive behaviour, I didn't feel any impulses anyhow, I was in turmoil. The last place I wanted to go was home, even though I knew in my heart and soul that it was inevitable that I would return, my mum needed looking after, she was getting more and more frail by the day. I was in no condition to look after her. I couldn't even look after myself.

Every now and then, I would get a phone call enquiring as to when I would come home. I was happy to stay in confinement, because I knew what was facing me at home, more depression, being imprisoned in the house, self imposed of course, trying to deal with the mundane stuff of everyday living and caring for my mum. I couldn't stand the thought of not having a routine, of not going to work, not going out on the hills, or on the bike, normal stuff I had taken for granted. Everyone seemed to have a sense of purpose, would come and visit and then take off to get on with their activities. I was the black sheep of the family.

I spent two weeks in the psychiatric unit; it seemed like two years, an interminably numbing experience. On the drive home, I looked up at the mountains from the passenger's seat of the car, the magnificent vista of the Reeks Range in all their splendour and I wondered to myself how the hell I was ever going to make it to those much loved hills again. I was physically wasted, in no condition to contemplate even a walk down the Port Road, nearby.

I was reluctant to move out of the house, to do the shopping, all the chores that had to be done; renew prescriptions, attend doctor's appointments, psychiatric appointments, it went on and on. That was the extent of my life. I hated not having a work routine, the normality of it, and the regularity. Time was moving excruciatingly slow for me. I had to appear to be somewhat normal to any visitors who called to the house. I hated that, I was in no mood for small talk, niceties, chin wagging.

I managed to take a walk one morning, only to meet my previous doctor who proceeded to tell me; "Get over it, ive seen a lot worse than you". That hammered me back down into the ground; all I wanted was a kind word, a nod of compassion and approval, however minute. I strayed off the track after that encounter, picked more remote walking areas. I wanted to be alone all of the time, mired in misery and hopelessness. I dreaded going shopping, inevitably bumping into people I didn't want to meet or confront, it was so painful. I had to look after my mum, and I struggled to cope with this alien routine of mine.

I would sleep very little, and in the mornings I would hear the rattling of the construction workers nearby, and I felt so guilty about not being able to go back to work, to contribute, to feel worthy again, and to feel human. It was humiliating.

I wasn't built for this kind of living, I was a high achiever, I needed to get out and do as everyone else seemed to be doing, getting on with their lives. I was an observer, looking on and wishing I could be part of the pack. Instead, I was barely able to surface in the mornings. I hadn't slept for a minute, my mind was in a sewer, regurgitating endlessly all those negative thoughts and episodes in my life where I had so many regrets, not being able to articulate my feelings properly and therefore removing me from so many rewarding opportunities, scuttling relationships along the way, notably my time with Karen and the missed opportunities there.

Of course the bully boy was foremost in my thoughts when I was inside in hospital, and when I got home, not a day would go by when I would ask myself; "why the hell did you not stop him"? Especially when I showed so much empathy to a lying son of a bitch who rolled me over in the gutter for years on end, then stamped me out lie a cockroach on his way out the door?

Yet again, a job would come in and as I didn't have the computer diagnostic skills, I would repeatedly ask him to come in and help. It was bit like Stockholm syndrome. I thought that this guy was really smart because he had very mediocre electrical skills, but behind it all he was a waffler, a bottom feeder, an asshole. He humiliated me repeatedly, never once said anything good about anyone or anything. I tormented myself about my naivety, in rolling over and taking all this crap.

Meanwhile, back home, I was tending to my mum and trying my best to come out of the black hole, but progress was very slow, especially with the environment I was in. I had to be available on demand, get her out of bed in one piece, go to the shops, make tea for any of the frequent callers, cook lunch, and repeat the procedure again and again. I couldn't see any way out of my predicament.

Any free time I had involved going to social services or psychiatric appointments in between doctors and chemists visits. We had two carers coming to the house, one in the mornings and one in the afternoon, for just half an hour or so. One of them spent most of the time chatting and drinking tea or charging her phone, rather than do any meaningful work around the place. But some were real angels of mercy; they couldn't do enough in the time allowed.

I went to the garden shed one morning and looked at my bike, wondering would I ever get back to the antics I had been doing for years on end, such enjoyment, such passion, such madness. The crazy falls I had taken on various single tracks, some involved concussion and were mildly insane. The night I was cycling out around Muckross and Dinis, on a very stormy and wet winter's night, with only a head torch for light. I was hammering around a bend when I hit a stags hind leg and stunned him, or the time I was on a GR7 route in Spain and it came to a sweeping fast downhill stretch with a little gully, where I arrived way too fast only to bash my head in a bad fall, I wondered aloud; "Where am I, Who am I"? Could I ever contemplate getting back to that level of fitness and nice madness ever again?

I had an old shopping bike that I used around town, it was an old Raleigh single speed woman's bike, but I loved it, I could leave it anywhere unlocked as nobody could possibly find it attractive in any way, but I did. I took it for a spin down to Ross castle and around the national park one morning. I found my legs were working fine, but I never considered the possibility of cycling in anger again, all the pain of it, heart pumping, lungs bursting, adrenaline production on a massive scale. I took it out more and more as time dragged by, but only for short spins around town mainly. I was overly conscious of the pain and soreness in my hands and wrists, and never tried to push myself too much. I had to get home as I had to attend to all the chores anyhow. On several occasions, I wanted to keep cycling, until I dropped, to numb the pain.

I took a terrible fall one morning, whilst rushing across to lidle for ice cream for my mum. I hit loose stones on the road and fell heavily on my right side, injuring my back badly. It took several weeks to recover from the fall, I wouldn't mind but I was only going 500 metres or so and it was against the grain for me. It said everything about my mental state at the time, lack of focus, inability to concentrate, impulsive behaviour again. But I did get the vanilla ice cream!

I gained more confidence from my cycling, and weeks later moved on to my regular mountain bike. Anytime I got on this bike, my mindset changed totally. It was now getting serious, I had to push on and attack at every opportunity, attack myself that is! It was me against the clock now, I couldn't just mosey around on this bike, and I was in full combat gear, except for the helmet. I wanted to escape to the mountain tracks, though I didn't plan it that way.

I headed on out the Kenmare road and when it came to the turn off for Torc Mountain, I couldn't resist. I headed off onwards and upwards, heart racing, head racing, and legs aching. Crossed the bridge on to the start of the old road to Kenmare, where there is a very steep upwards climb that would try the best mountain bikers. I came across another mountain biker half way up the climb, his chain had broken, and I helped him to fix it and got him going again. I was very pleased with myself, I felt satisfied that I had got someone out of a hole, however small it may have been. He had gone well ahead as I struggled to get up the hill, but I wanted to catch him and pass him of course. It came to very open ground with very fast descent into narrow sleepers over a little stream. I barrelled down the hill flat out only for my front wheel to lodge between the sleepers and I went flying over the handlebars onto my face, splitting my nose and forehead, bloodied but unbowed. I was stunned like that stag I hit previously, concussed yet again.

An accident always happens in slow motion. Every single detail of the impact is recorded in miniscule detail. The milli second before the impact, I could count the stones on the ground, tell their structure, see the life in the trickling water under the sleepers, measure the gap between the sleepers. As I looked up, I saw the approaching cyclist I had just passed like a bat out of hell, and I asked him how I looked, did I need stitches? I think he was more stunned than I, was unresponsive, and ambled on. I took a quick look at my bike and after a few adjustments, cycled back the way I had come, blood trickling down my face, black and blue with bruising. I went straight to the doctors, and she sent me over to A @ E as I required stitching and I had damaged a tendon in my right hand. I was more concerned about the damage done to the bike, but it survived, only just.

That accident kept me quiet for a while, though not for long. As I couldn't cycle, there was always the mountain, and I would try and get back to walking fitness in the following weeks. Like everything of this nature, small steps are required before moving onwards and upwards. I always loved steep ground, especially rocky wet gullies, where any progress was made by deftly stepping on to various cracks in the rock to move upwards and onwards. The more challenging the move, the bigger the thrill, especially if there was ice and snow on the rock. On numerous occasions, I had left it too late to put on my crampons on steep icy ground, thereby exposing myself to a possible fall, but that was part of the buzz, wasn't it? I loved those days out, just me and the mountain, no meaningless banter or mundane conversations to listen to.

I ventured out into the mountains soon enough. The cycling helped my fitness, but my legs were lacking the build up of muscle tone required for serious mountain running. I went up Mangerton Mountain first, to test my fitness, and I was going nicely. Part of the rehabilitation therapy involved planning numerous activities, and carrying them out as such, no more impulsive behaviour. I would write down a list of activities for the week ahead and I would have to do each one as listed, in order to get some regularity back in to my life, reasons to be cheerful I suppose.

After a number of trips up Mangerton in one week, I said I'd head back to the Mcgillycuddy Reeks, my stomping ground for as long as I can remember. Mentally, I was in no condition to be out, I was still full of anger, frustration and rage, with myself and the world at large.

I started out up the Hags Glen taking it gently but firmly. I went to the top of The Heavenly Gates, from where you start the climb up Howling Ridge. It was a wet and windy day, the rock was very slippery. I managed to make the summit with no hassle, but when I was on top, there was a huge crowd there, and in my state of mind at the time, I just wanted it to be quiet and peaceful. I got a mad fit whilst on the summit, and as I looked over at the Beenkeragh Ridge, I said to myself that id run across the top of the ridge and go on to Knockbrinnea and down to the car.

This was one of my favourite walks for years, but as I reached Beenkeragh, I met another large group just off the summit, and that drove me to run myself into the ground for the remaining 3k or so. I ran down from knockbrinnea like a lunatic, pushing myself way beyond the pain barrier with no regard for my physical well being. Normally on that kind of decent, I would start slowly, but this time I went hell for leather from the summit down to the car, I wanted my heart to stop, to end the pain. Instead, I got the worst dose of shin splints that you could imagine, my knees were painful all of the time and the pain running down along my shin bone was unbearable, it curtailed my walking for a long time afterwards.

I tortured myself yet again, for not being more measured, for not looking after myself. This would have serious consequences for me, as it was my only outlet from all the mundane stuff at home, and I was falling back into despair and psychotic behaviour again. I was a loose canon, ready to explode, my own worst enemy. I spent days sitting in the car listening to the radio, looking up at the mountains, wishing I could break out at any moment and take off for the nearest summit. I had sabotaged myself again, sabotaged my legs, those legs had taken so much abuse from me over the years, and here I was trying to break them, after all the enjoyment they gave me.

The lack of routine was slowly killing me inside, the laborious shopping routines, the constant appointments with the Mental Health services, I had no respite. Family members would visit on weekends, and it drove me crazy to see them going back on the Sunday night, back to their jobs and loved ones, back to a normal life, the freedom of it. I felt like a prisoner in my own home with no escape.

I was at breaking point again a year later, after all this trauma. I jumped in the car and drove to Allihies in West Cork, a place that I had spent some of the happiest times of my life, with Karen years earlier, and with friends, where we would go mountain biking and walking by the sea, take a boat trip and on the way back call in to Teddy's in Killmac for a pint. I didn't know what I was doing.

I drove down to Ballydonegan pier; it was very stormy, the wild Atlantic waves breaking over the rocky outcrops. I walked up to the cliffs nearby, where years previously, I had spent so many happy hours rock climbing on the sea cliffs, routes like "Tralee Dog Show" or "Babooshka", with the surf breaking bellow you, the sun at your back, the pumping adrenaline required to move on to the next crack, totally invigorating stuff. Yet here was I, looking down at the same cliffs, wondering whether it would be better for everyone if I jumped. The sea didn't look inviting, the rocks neither. It looked very cold. I walked on along the cliffs, had another look down, no, this was not the right spot either.

I walked back to the car and drove to Allihies, which was eerily quiet and calm, all it was missing was the tumbleweed blowing through the main street. I continued on up to the Copper Mines, a very steep road a couple of miles high up above the village. I reached the summit of the hill where the road is unpaved and very gravelly. I tried to turn the car around, but the rear wheels got stuck in a drain and I couldn't move the car, I was stuck fast, blocking the road. I tried to horse the car around but only managed to crease the rear quarter panel, it was very light.

I soon realised that I had no means of escape, so I spent the whole night in the car or walking around the area and drinking bog water out of the ground. I found a box of roses chocolates in the back seat and chewed them endlessly. I was hallucinating late into the night and I saw leprechauns approaching from the village with their head torches alight. In fact, they were locals from the village who had spotted my stranded car and came up to investigate proceedings. They came no closer than 20 metres and then retreated back down to the village, whist I just stood and stared at them nonchalantly. The early morning seemed to take so long to come and it wasn't until 12pm that a van drove up from the village and towed me out of the stream and set me on my way.

The Good Samaritan got my car facing the right direction, and off I went, with no destination in mind. I drove into every cul de sac around Eyeries, got out of the car briefly, took a few steps, and then got back in the car. I didn't want to go back home. I pulled off the main road after Lauragh village, and tried to get 40 winks. I was exhausted, physically and mentally.

I saw a car coming up the road and I watched him turn around and come back towards me. It was a garda, I was on the missing list and the gardai were notified. I drove off in the Kenmare direction, conscious of the fact that I was being followed. I drove lively enough; hoping to turn off to lose my pursuer, but there was no turn off I could see, so I pulled in to a lay by and stopped. There was a garda car coming the other way and they spotted my car, came over to me and tried to assure me that I was in safe hands. I was in a tormented state, as they drove me back to Kenmare and gave me tea and biscuits, before calling someone from home to collect me.

I was back in the Looney bin again, spent another couple of weeks there, horrendous though the thought was. I didn't want to leave, I was increasingly psychotic, I figured I had blown it again. I just couldn't handle the mind numbing routine at home, no prospect of a bit of cheer or light heartedness; it was all too serious and negative for me. I was operating like a machine, going through the motions, no prospects of advancement. I felt I had nothing to contribute, as nobody engaged me in any serious conversation, after all I had a "condition", and no one would believe anything I said, except for the odd patronising comment. It was also convenient for everyone else in the family to have me at home, I was kept in my place, this was my job now, get used to it.

I often wondered what happens when we kill ourselves, would we end up in that burning furnace that is hell, with no prospect of salvation, no reward for suffering so much earthly torment ? Would we be tormented souls forever, never to find peace? It is, after all, seen by many as the easy way out, an escape, an irresponsible and selfish act. Try telling that to someone who is so traumatised that they cannot see any respite in this world, so they may as well end it all in a brief moment of madness, never to be repeated.

It broke my heart to see everyone getting on with their lives, mine was on hold for the foreseeable future, I had no outlet left. I was sent by the mental health services to a rehab institute in Killarney, where you could learn gardening, wood work, art and basic living skills, cooking and so on. It took me a while to get into it, but digging the soil was so lovely, turning over the sod, planting vegetables and spuds was very soulful work, very rewarding.

The art was a different story, it took me a long time to get the hang of it and when it came to picking out a picture to paint, I picked the most difficult one, a lovely waterfall, running down between trees and multi coloured boulders, splashing into a pool at the base. It took me 3 months to complete it, but when finished, I was gobsmacked when I came back after a few days and looked at the finished work. Of course I was never happy with the final result, it took me back to my work days when I would always look for the faintest flaw in a completed job, always saying to myself; "could have done better".

Summer was approaching, and I was offered a chance to go on a cycling trip to Santiago De Compostella in The Basque country in Northern Spain. The idea was to cycle the route from the starting point of St Jean Da Port, 800 km in 9 days. I didn't want to go at first, as I wasn't mentally fit for it, not to mention the physical aspect of it. It is one of the most famous pilgrimages in Europe, with various starting points. The patron Saint was St James, and James's Gate in Dublin where Arthur Guinness signed his 10,000 year lease, was the real starting point.

We flew out to Biarritz in France, before catching a train to our starting point, St Jean. The heat was stifling, this was August after all, and only mad dogs and Irish men go out in the mid day sun, never mind cycling in 40 degree heat. We carried any spare clothing on a carrier as we travelled light. The Basque country was stunning, the heat lovely, after firstly acclimatising to it. I didn't have time to think, such was the pace and intensity of the trip. It was the perfect place to find peace and tranquillity, but not at our rate of progress.

The first day of the cycle from St Jean was uphill mostly for most of the morning. I never spent as much time in first gear on the granny ring on a bike. People were walking past us we were going so slowly, the climb was relentless. Once you reached a flat section, it only lasted briefly until the next climb; it went on for six hours or so and we had covered around 40k in all that time. The Pico mountain range looked stunning in the early morning, but we stopped only for a few minutes along the way to take on water, as we were running the risk of dehydration in the heat of the day.

I could have done with just walking the whole route, taking my own time trying to banish my demons. Instead, they were on the back of the bike, pushing me on yet again. I didn't have time to catch my breath during the whole trip. We were in the lovely city of Pamplona, famous for the running with the bulls, when I took a stroll around, looking down from the very high walls surrounding the city, and thought about how painful it would be to jump off the wall, sabotaging the whole trip for the others. I needed a pilgrimage more than anyone, but I was back on the bandwagon again, trying to prove myself, being called "l' animal" on numerous occasions along the route by the walkers.

The whole trip to Spain passed in a flash; I even got my calf branded, after inadvertedly rubbing it off the red hot brake disc on the bike, after a particularly steep descent. My leg was branded with the imprint for months after. It was my legacy of the trip.

I went to see my rheumatologist in Cork soon after the Spanish trip, he takes one look at me and says; "You've been busy"? Sarcastically of course. I could have stolen the conrods out of his lovely BMW 335 on my way out afterwards, he was so fucken smug, especially when he proceeded to inject my knees without even explaining what was in the syringe and why I needed it! Oh tis just an anti-inflammatory. Jesus help me with consultants! I changed consultants after that faux pa.

Back home, things didn't get much better, it was only temporary relief. I was back on the dull treadmill, the boring routine, the constant battle with myself trying to cope as best I could. The best I could have hoped for was a brief respite at the weekend, going to the pub, meeting a few friends. If I was an alcoholic, I would have drunk myself to death.

I made an appointment with a psychiatrist privately, as the mental health service had a 12 month waiting period. I made good progress with him. He tried re-programming therapy, which involved modifying my thinking, or rebooting my hard drive. A lot of stuff I couldn't face, I was scared to look at it. I had become immune to the abuse, but inevitably, it was chipping away at me, I couldn't escape from its clutches.

Years and years of psychological abuse took their toll, which is why I didn't want to go there. I refused to admit to myself that I was so naïve, and vulnerable to abuse of this kind. After numerous sessions, I was diagnosed with post traumatic stress disorder. Now that is mainly associated with soldiers working on the front line in places like Iraq or Afghanistan, where they are exposed to the most inhumane treatment one can imagine. Yet, here was I, in no way associated with war or conflict, being driven into the ground on numerous occasions by a terrible bully. I tormented myself for years for not being able to confront him, it had gone on far too long and I was powerless to act.

As I looked deeper into the humiliation and abuse, I was able to open the door into that horrible room, that room full of skeletons that I was afraid to open. It was torture to recall even brief images of the humiliation I was subjecting myself to. It was like trying to close a door with a wall of water behind it, let it all in and I was drowning, no hope of rescue. But let in a trickle at a time and I could deal with it.

After the sessions I would go over every detail in my head, making it even more difficult to find peace of mind. However, it was working, and I was feeling better about myself, my ability to banish the ghost out of my life. I still felt a terrible emptiness within; the self destruct button was there by my side, willing and able to offer a permanent solution.

Those sessions were my lifeline; my target was to make each appointment on the prescribed day. In between appointments, I mulled over my inability to look into the closet, the toll it was taking on my mental health. Survival was the only mode I knew for that period, I was just existing, going through the motions.

One of my favourite cycles had always been back to Puck, or Killorglin as it is known as. But along the back road to Puck lived my tormentor. I would approach the area like a sniper, trying to get past as fast as possible. It was like cycling through a minefield, such was my fear and torment, and more so since the recent psychology sessions. I dreaded coming across him.

During the therapy, I brought up the subject of murder. I figured I would only get 4 years or so in jail for manslaughter. It would be a crime of passion, with extenuating circumstances. Also, I would have gotten on -going psychotherapy in jail, instead of rifling into my little piggy bank. However, I desisted, got on with my therapy in the hope of one day finding peace and contentment in my life. It was a living hell; I could see no light at the end of the tunnel. I had to stop the sessions eventually, as I couldn't afford them on a continual basis, but I learned how to approach the topic with the mind training I was taught. I had learnt a good lesson.

My self esteem hovered between normal to rock bottom, depending on my own ability to make progress, however minute. I still felt like an outcast, could never get used to being unemployed, absolutely zero dignity. I hated going to the social welfare services begging for survival money, money I laughed at for years before, especially so in the run up to Christmas, when a bonus payment of 10 Euros would be paid. It was torture for me, going through the whole undignified process.

My saviour was again the great outdoors, I always loved getting out in the mountains, and now I had another chance to do things at a more normal pace. Previously, I would have run myself into the ground on a regular basis; I didn't know what it meant to take it easy. My work was like that too, where I would work myself into a lather of sweat until the job was finished. I could relax afterwards, in the knowledge I had done a good days work in half a day.

Despite the entire trauma, I still had a sense of humour; I could see the funny side of life as it was. When I was in the psychiatric unit in Tralee, I was walking around outside in the tiny concrete garden, when this woman walked straight into me ranting; "that's my line you're walking on", or when I walked past the ECT room, I would picture the event taking place in more light-hearted circumstances, like putting a so called normal person through the ECT shock therapy. Maybe they would turn the other way? There is good madness and bad, and I suffered on the positive side, though the negatives tried their best to beat the positives, but to no avail. You can't keep a madman down, well not for long.

Slowly, I was making progress, learning how to cope with my broken life. Numerous times I would pass various garages and look in at the industriousness of the place, the work ethic that is survival for most people, the dignity of walking away on a Friday evening with a pay packet for a job well done, or otherwise. That could have been me, I would say to myself, tormenting behaviour. Yet, when I was working inside these places, I felt like a prisoner, looking out at the mountains , and wished I was climbing some rocky outcrop, adrenaline pumping, straining at the leash to move on to the next technical step.

Self flagellation couldn't go on anymore, I was sick to the teeth of it, it was getting monotonous and boring, and I was beginning to lose all those lovely quirky personality traits that I had for years. If I had any hope of living a normal life I had to bring all this thinking to a halt, otherwise I would lose contact with the real world, that beautiful world that had offered me so many opportunities to enjoy all its splendour, the countless times I had taken off on a whim into the hills or ventured on yet another mad cycle trip, the intoxication of it all.

I would have to put bed all the negative episodes in my life, all the torment I had suffered from the bullies of this world, I was after all, better than all of those. I still had much to offer, but only if I got over this huge mountain of torment in my soul. Yes, I was a broken man, my own worse enemy, but I was the only one able to offer a solution. No psychotherapist can instil self belief and confidence in you if you cannot figure it out in your own mind. No medication can provide the final solution. No amount of approval seeking or endorsements of goodwill from others can help. Perceptions have to change, expectations and value systems have to alter, pride and ego have to be thrown out the window, and the rear view mirror in the car has to be discarded, what's behind is of no further consequence, its now time to move on from the rubble, to start building again. The engine management light is finally extinguished, hopefully for good, inevitably only for brief periods of calm.

I couldn't think straight when I was at home all the time, caring for my mum. It was like my outside life never existed beyond the front door. One weekend morning, I awoke as usual for the 8 am ritual of getting her out of bed and onto the toilet. However, on this particular weekend, we had family staying over for the weekend and I thought someone else would do the morning chore, to relieve me for one morning. To my horror, I heard a loud thud coming from the bathroom, mum had taken a heavy fall, and when I entered the bathroom what greeted me was pure horror.

The poor woman had decided for once, to go to the toilet unaided, to her detriment. She had fallen on her right side, breaking her hip and cutting her head in the fall. There was blood weeping from the head wound, she was faint and in total disarray. As she lay on the ground I tried to comfort her, sat her on the floor, whilst not moving her in case of injuring her even more. I felt faint, a cold sweat rolled down my body, I froze with the shock for a minute or so.

There was further panic when the others were summoned to the bathroom, we were like headless chickens. The doctor was summonsed and an ambulance was dispatched, whilst the delay seemed interminably long, though in reality it was only 20 minutes or so. I wanted to throw up, but couldn't, I felt so helpless and inadequate in the face of such a crisis. Once she was lifted off the floor and put on to a stretcher, there was a brief respite. Here was I again, lambasting myself for not getting to her as usual, as was my routine every morning, but this particular morning no one was responsible for getting her up out of bed. I was thrown back into turmoil again, there was a long road to recovery yet again, and I didn't know if either of us would be able for it.

My mum always had fears about ending up in accident and emergency, the indignity of it, the coldness, the pain, the long waiting hours on a trolley, waiting for a bed. This would be an enormous setback for her and for everyone in the family. She had osteoporosis as well, complicating the surgery even more, and she often spoke of her fears of being left to die in terrible circumstances with no dignity or kindness. It was total humiliation for her.

This whole experience had a devastating affect on me; I was reliving those terrible scenarios in my own mind, even more so because of my continuing fight against that black dog, always lurking in the background, threatening me at every opportunity, willing me to get into that black hole again. It was like the bully boy, kicking me constantly when I was down, or even when I was upbeat. There would always be that sly negative comment on his way out the door, a kick up the arse just in case you might feel good about yourself and your work.

I was back on auto pilot again, going through the motions, over and back to the hospital, wondering how was I going to be able to cope with this latest drama. Mum was very resilient, especially considering her latest traumas. I suppose faith had a lot to do with it, but she always managed to calm the situation with the exclamation; "sure tis gods will". Gods will maybe, but I felt responsible in a way for putting her in that hospital due to my negligence, my inability to keep to the schedule as it worked, my failure yet again. Here we go again, not again.

She got through the surgery very well, despite our worries. The problem now was deciding where she would go, who would look after her. She got a bed in the local hospital near us, and as time went by, she became very depressed with her situation, her inability to walk, her high dependency. At certain times, I sensed that she had thrown in the towel. She didn't want to eat, her face was constantly down, and responses were mournful. There was no life in her. It was very difficult to see her in those circumstances, painful in fact. She had given up the ghost. As the weeks dragged on, things didn't improve much. There was no stimulation or any kind of therapy in the hospital, it was a respite home really, attended to the basic functions one needed, that's all.

I was fighting a losing battle again, I hated to see mum in that condition, she didn't deserve it. She was always kind to everyone, the kettle was always on standby in case anyone called. All her life she was afraid to leave the house in case she would miss any callers. If Osama Bin Laden was at the door, she would ask him did he want a cup of tea and a fresh scone, in between going to the front line!

Yet, here she was, thrown to the mercy of our health services, with their endlessly frustrating beaurocracy and lack of compassion. From now on the shoe was on the other foot, it was form filling, applications for a place in a nursing home, the family silver was going to be raided, apocalypse. I started to polish the silverware just in case it might be useful. It went on and on for months and months. I felt I was out on a ledge with no safety rope. There was no way up or down. We were thrown to the wolves of the system; they would do a forensic trawl of income and assets, in the hope that we had something in reserve to tie us over this very demanding schedule.

Eventually, a bed was obtained in a lovely nursing home near Killarney, not far from town. Of course the thought of it was enough to send mum into more depression, she would be out of her comfort zone, her own home. She failed to see any bright side to the move; it was all doom and gloom, a downwards spiral to ignominy and death. It was like pulling hens teeth, trying to convince her as to the positives of the move, no, she wanted to be in her own bed at home, end of story.

As time went by, the room was slowly transformed into a beautiful homely room, with her own personal effects and decorations, old photographs of her wedding day, where she looked stunningly beautiful, to a cabinet topped out with cards from well wishers, mass bouquets from all the "Corn Buns" (nuns) who must have drunk a tanker load of tea and a juggernaut full of fresh scones over the years in our house. It was one of the perks of being a nun or a priest, you were treated like royalty, the china cups and saucers were taken down, the porcelain tea pot was deployed, and the oven was on slow burn for the perfect scone, not to mention the gorgeous jams on offer. I sometimes wished I was a priest as I would be fated till the cows came home, but we had no cows!

I used to get a great laugh at some of the nuns attempts to drive off afterwards. First gear was alien to some, the clutch was only a nuisance of a pedal, and in fact launch control systems would have suited them perfectly. You put your life in their hands if taking a lift to town, as I would have goten there faster in my shopping bike, and without the inevitable tail back of cars behind , their drivers indignant with rage, trying to overtake them. Mechanical sympathy wasn't high on their list; it was in the lap of the gods. I remember in particular, one winter's eve, seeing this elderly nun overtaking a line of cars over the continuous white line, with no apparent hope of pulling it off, with oncoming cars pulling over and flashing their headlights with venom, but on she pushed, it was her line, no discussions, no contest.

My poor Aunty Nora's health was declining at this time also. She was placed in a nursing home in Tralee for some years prior to her death. I made a habit of visiting Sr Nora; well I couldn't ignore her, as I would get frequent phone calls inquiring as to what day I would be over and I was always reluctant to name the day or the particular time, as I was working, and if it was quiet at work, I would rush over to see her for a quick visit. Poor Nora suffered form TIA's, or "Transient Ischemic Attacks", where the supply of blood is interrupted on its way to the brain, thereby causing mini-strokes. She would frequently call me and say "Ger, will you come over in the morning, I think I'm going to die tomorrow." You would want to be a cruel individual by not responding to this ultimatum, but it went on for around 15 years or so until her death.

It was painful to visit the nursing home in the early stages as you would be met with the retort; "please take me home to my own bed"; it was very distressing at first, but gradually a realisation came in that she could no longer be cared for at home. But still she persisted with the thought that this was only a temporary accommodation, it would pass in time. What was particularly hard to take was one day when a priest visited her and commented openly; "sure Gerard could look after you at home", I felt like disembowelling him, the insensitivity of the man, after all the trouble in trying to settle her in.

Nursing homes are strange places, lots of people dread going into them, afraid to confront the ultimate reality that we may all need one sometime or other. People's souls are exposed in the nursing home, after all, what have you have left when you can no longer wash yourself, feed yourself, or go to the toilet unaided? It's the ultimate nightmare scenario for most people. You are seemingly at the mercy of total strangers, people of all nationalities, coming together with a common purpose, to ease the pathway at the doors of heaven. People may have Alzheimer's or one of the countless involuntary conditions, but I have met some of the nicest people in there, who speak from the soul, who are not afraid of death in its many guises, who try with every last grain to keep the little dignity they have left in the face of overwhelming odds.

I would rather die with my boots on rather than end up in a nursing home, but we don't have the final say. Some day I may be grateful for the facility. Meanwhile, I will carry on as best I can and keep moving as much as possible, preferably forwards!

I'm back on the bike one stormy afternoon, one particularly stressful day when mum has developed pneumonia and I am really tired from the hours spent at the home. I had to get out in the air, so I do a short trip of 25k, and coming back down the Killarney bypass, I'm almost home, just approaching the roundabout on the cycle lane which ends up where you have to mount the footpath and avoid the traffic light pole. My glasses are wet and fogged up, and with my bit of double vision I misjudge the pole by inches, crashing my shoulder against the pole and falling out onto the path of the fast approaching traffic flat on my back.

I instinctively get up quickly, but there is a terrible crunching sound in my shoulder, I know something is broken or fractured. I get back on the bike and slowly make it home. I go straight to A @ E in Tralee, wait for a couple of hours to get to a doctor, and have an x- ray. A fractured collar bone was diagnosed, requiring just a sling and a long wait for rehabilitation. The following morning, I was out on the bike, using a prussik for support, and went back to Puck, taking my hand off the sling occasionally, but making good time despite my injury. Unihanded cycling was a synch, apart from the inconvience and the pain. It wasn't going to get in my way, even though I was told to keep it on a sling for 6 weeks. I couldn't sit around all day without getting out on the bike or heading to the hills, so I brought the home made sling with me for support.

Back in the nursing home, mums condition was critical, and it came to decision time. In order to get intravenous antibiotics administered, she would have to be admitted to hospital in Tralee, as the nursing home was not allowed to do this. She declined, saying that she would rather die in her bed, surrounded by family, rather than suffering the indignity of being in A @ E again. The doctor held out no hope of recovery without this intervention, but miraculously she fought her way out of it and recovered fully in a week or so. The doctor couldn't believe her resilience, her fighting spirit. We all expected the worst and we were gobsmacked when the pneumonia disappeared.

Chapter 5

As Good As It Gets

I'm camping on the Great Blasket Island in the mid eighties. I pick out a nice little site, overlooking the famous White Strand and only a stones throw from a lovely little white washed cottage with its tarred roof. As I am camping for a week, I get to know one Paddy Dunleavy, a retired school teacher, who spent the month of August every year in his baptismal home. He stands at the gate of the cottage, looking out on all the people disembarking from the ferry on their day trip around the island. He tells me that he's sick and tired of those bloody Yanks coming up to him and asking him to pose for a photo, a memento of their trip. He wished that they would leave him alone, in peace.

In the evenings, I call down to the cottage and Paddy invites me in. We sit by the turf fire, listening to Radio Na Gaeltachta, sipping bottles of Guinness, ranting and raving about our day. As he is running low on Guinness, I take the ferry across to the mainland where I have to buy food for the few days and I bring a few six packs for Paddy as well.

A couple of nights later, I pop in to meet Paddy and he asks me if I'm going to the party on Inishvickillane, Charles Haughey's sanctuary. Apparently, it was Charlie's birthday that weekend and Paddy said to come along as a friend of his, sure nobody would no any different! He said to be at the pier at 7pm that evening, when the boat would be arriving from the mainland. The party had started hours earlier in Kruger Kavanagh's pub over in Dunquin and from there they took the regular ferry across, stopping to pick us up on their way.

As we waited on the pier for the boat, there were a few Italian tourists waiting to get back to the mainland on the last boat. However, when the boat docked, the skipper told the Italians that he had to make a short journey to another island before returning for them. There was a guy playing the fiddle on the boat and people were dancing and singing, the Italians couldn't believe there eyes. We got on board and made our way to Inishvickillane in a descending fog and docked at the rocky little slipway on to the island.

We made our way up the very steep ground, until we came to a plateau, whereupon good old Charlie appeared like a visionary missionary, with his arms outstretched, welcoming all and sundry to his lair. As he filtered through the guests, he looked at me and asks me who I am and where did I come from. I noted a sudden alienation at this inquisition, so I just told him that Paddy was a friend of mine. He reluctantly left me through, though I felt uneasy and an unwelcome addition to his guest list. We made our way up to his sumptuous cottage with its lovely native stone, apparently sourced from the island.

The dining room was the piece de resistance, with huge candelabras and a ceiling crafted from huge oak trees that were felled in a storm at his Georgian estate in Kinsealy. It had to have been hurricane Charlie! Many of the guests were locals form Dingle, who had constructed the house over the previous years, and legend had it that one day, they discovered the wine cellar with its collection of vintage and rare wines, and proceeded to drink most of the wine, replacing it with cheap bottles of wine bought in a supermarket in Dingle. This man was our Taoiseach at the time, the man entrusted with running our country. God help us and save us said old Mrs Davis!

Everyone was shteaving drunk at the party and at one stage someone got on the shipping VHF radio and made contact with a trawler from Valentia that happened to be fishing in the area, and invited them up for a drink. Come early morning, the said fishermen had to be physically ejected from the party as they were gone mad with drink. They were carried out in a comatose state, and how they ever got back to the trawler, never mind getting behind the helm, was baffling to me, especially as the morning was very foggy.

Charlie himself acted out his role as the country squire to perfection, he truly believed that his ancestors were chieftains and landed gentry, and he figured himself as belonging to a different class. He introduced red deer to his island hideaway and was very protective of his privacy. The man could surely party!

We slept on the floor in the dining room, as we had to wait for the boat to get us back to the Great Blasket in the morning. The boat departed at 7 am in a thick fog, patrons with sore heads and stomachs. As we approached the Blasket, I could see three people waving their hands in the air with fury. It was the Italians from the previous night, they had stayed on the island all night with no camping or any other gear whatsoever, they were furious. What madness!

I'm after summiting Cotopaxi in Ecuador, with my umbilical rope attached to my guide. It is a stunningly beautiful morning, very cold, with great visibility across the plains of Ecuador. I don't stay too long at the summit, just enough time to take a few photos, as im getting cold, very cold. I want to get off the Mountain fast, to warm up and sweat it out. I am walking gingerly in front of Mani, my guide. I break into a run with my crampons on, but find them restricting me, eventually one of them flies off my shoe and I stop briefly and put it in to my rucksack, continue on running with one crampon, now pulling my guide behind me, he's laughing at me but after 45 minutes or so he's tired and beckoning me to slow down. I don't, he's acting like a moving belay for me as I descend like a lunatic, skiing on boots down to the hut, and I can't wait to take off the rope. Both of us are exhausted when we arrive at the hut, I go to bed for an hour to recover, before moving on down the mountain. Splendid madness, this is as good as it gets.

Back in the nursing home, these poor creatures would love to go for a stroll out around the grounds if they were able, with their little three wheeled trolleys they use for support, every step is infinitely more daring than any technical ice climb anywhere in the world. Just looking at their faces after hobbling around the car park fills me with wonder, so much reward for so much effort. It is a brief triumph over adversity for them, one small step for mankind, one large step for the soul. It is invigorating to see. They may as well have topped out on Everest.

Families are strange when it comes down to the wire, for the hard decisions to be made; no one wants to commit their parents into a nursing home. No one wants to be committed to a mental hospital, voluntarily or otherwise. Lip service is paid by lots of people, to appear to the outside world that they are considerate and unselfish, but ultimately, in this world, it's every man for himself, or woman.

I'm sea kayaking from Dunquin out to the Blasket islands; I'm trying out a sea kayak for the first time, having previously used a plastic canoe. I find it very difficult to balance the boat, and after a while I take a roll, 500 metres out from the harbour, I manage to get into the boat and paddle on out to sea, but capsize again further out. Im pissed off now as I think im ruining the trip for the others, and one of them tows me back to land and I get the plastic boat which I am used to and rejoin the paddle. The swells are huge as I lose sight of the others, but regain it again as the swells drop. I am making great progress considering my poor boat and lack of experience in these conditions. The tide is against us and it is a struggle to point the boat in the right direction, but we make good headway out to the white strand on the Great Blasket. What an invigorating trip.

I meet some lovely individuals in the nursing home; Ed is an American man, who was a welder in a boatyard in New Jersey for most of his working life. He shuffles up and down the corridor with his little frame for support; he's a proper gentleman, loves taking a smoke in the little room at the end of the corridor. He regales his years in New Jersey, the hard work of the welder; he is very gently spoken, likes watching GAA championship matches, has no time for soccer, but is always in good form.

There's John C, who could be a male model such is his immaculate dress every time I see him, with his little peaked cap and repetitive chant about "dirty water", the subject of which I am transfixed. I have surmised so far, that a calf was born in a field near dirty water, with all the surrounding dramas, no cup to make tea what with the dirty water. The poor man has Alzheimer's, but I could listen to him contentedly for an age, trying to decode what he is saying, it is intriguing to me. The conversation goes on to describe the "slatted units that were built with no pay, no pay". His accent is music to my ears, like poetry in motion. This man has magic on board.

I am cycling out from Thamel in Kathmandu, with a group of people just back from a trek to Everest Base camp. As we have a couple of days to kill, I look for victims to go mountain biking in the Kathmandu Valley, with one of the most hospitable guides I have ever met anywhere in the world. His name is Akshya, otherwise known as Ox. He supplies everything including a packed lunch for 30 dollars a day. He is priceless, has a natural flair with people, so full of life and that innocent beauty that us westerners have lost. Nothing fazes him, we stop at peoples houses along the valley, have tea and nourishment, but he supplies the best nourishment of all, coming from his heart and soul, it is so refreshing to see.

It brings me back to when I met Karen for the first time and how she became attracted to me; I was that person years previously, an open heart, a lovely innocence, and living life to the full every day. But life had become too complicated along the way. I lost that innocence in the face of an increasingly ravenous society, people never satisfied with their lot, upgrade was the byword, everyone wanted an upgrade, whether it was mobile phone, a new car, a plasma TV or a bigger house. I'd have been happy living in a cave on a mountain, the ultimate Ape.

Every year around the end of December, I remember Karen, and her inner beauty, that long lost love that I left behind. It was in December when we were supposed to marry, and it is like an anniversary for me, albeit shared quietly and covertly in my mind. The fantastic days we had spent driving from Cork airport to Killarney in the red corvette, often stopping at the Mills in Ballyvourney, where she would laugh heartily at the banter of the local farmers coming in chatting and ranting about nothing in particular, such lovely madness. One time on our descent from the County bounds, the red corvette said it was doing "The Ton" on the clock, with Karen urging me on to test its limits. Not bad for 957cc's!

One weekend in Allihies, we were in a pub where a few locals had assembled and Karen couldn't get over the accents, was astonished with the lovely quirky responses, the mining history in the village, its fascinating connections with Butte in Montana, when I'm brought back to my school days and the enormously challenging trek over the snowy mountains and on to the gold rush territory of Klondike. I was always fascinated by those exploits, it hit home to me the passion of the outdoors, the bravery of those poor souls, the suffering they went through in order to make some kind of a life for themselves and their families back home. I wanted to be one of them.

Sheila is struggling to walk down the corridor, she is partly blind, is constantly calling out "please help me, please help me," to all and sundry, night and day. It is gut wrenching to listen to and to observe a woman totally at the mercy of the carers, her soul totally exposed, her vulnerability obvious. She never seems to settle, even at night when I call, I can hear the same tormented voice, so heart wrenching.

I feel so helpless in the face of all this, I want to get out, and be glad that I am able to wander out under my own steam. But I cannot let myself out because there is an electronic door and someone has to come to open it. It seems like I am waiting for hours sometimes, when in fact it's only minutes. I always had a fear of being locked in somewhere, unable to get free. I used to dread staying in houses where security seemed to be unreal, multiple door locks, windows locked to fend off burglars, it was like staying in a prison. I couldn't breathe in these places and I always checked my escape route beforehand.

I am driving from San Francisco out to Pacific highway 1, on a beautiful sunny morning in my pocket rocket Mazda. It is a very challenging road, fast sweeping turns and a billiard table surface. I look in the rear view mirror and see 20 or so Hogs out on their Sunday morning run. They are going hell for leather, like bats out of hell. They overtake me one by one. I let them go, for a minute, before launching a rear gun action picking them off one by one until I get to the last one. He is getting nervous about my progress, keeps checking his rear view mirrors, but I'm not giving up until I subjugate him, silence him with my own spectacular backfire from my rotary engined powerhouse. He gives in, reluctantly, has a stunned look on his face as I pass like he was standing still. I smirk at myself, "take that lads", enjoying every minute of it. I stop and go for a swim in the Pacific blue warm water, what lovely madness.

I'm having a chat with a woman in the psychiatric unit, she has been here for months, is seriously ill. Topic of conversation is the Swiss Euthanasia clinic, where for a fee; they can assist you to make a final break, no frills attached. We discuss the pros and cons, finally concluding that it would be better than being stuck in this kip indefinitely, with no prospect of recovery, less so the longer you are here. Institutionalisation comes to mind, I had seen it over the years, people surrendered to mental homes for most of their adult lives, becoming unable to function in the outside world to any degree. Lots of these people were just surplus to requirements in their own homes, unwanted trash, not to be recycled. For Gods sake I was feeling like that after two fucken weeks, never mind years of confinement.

I am in the White Mountains in New Hampshire; it's my first time in the USA, in the late seventies. I had previously met a woman from Boston back in Cork, and I was smitten. She invited me over and we end up going to a ski cabin for the weekend with a few of her pals. This is my first attempt to ski, and as the rest of the party are experienced, I spend the first couple of hours on the nursery slopes, but eventually I join the others, onto a black run, it's very icy, full of gullies and moguls.

I spend more time on my arse than on the skis, as I cannot turn, and crash into a few trees along the way, but I survive, black and blue all over, but feel a great sense of achievement. I am physically exhausted afterwards; sleep it off after numerous beers, lovely madness.

Back in Boston, I meet her gorgeous sister and I ask her does she want to come on a drive down to Florida for few days, I want to go on a road trip in a Pontiac Transam, the ultimate muscle car. I phone some rental companies, but find it impossible to get a Transam, and I end up with a big spongy piece of Detroit metal, it's like a ship, rolling all over the place. I abort the trip and return the car to the rental people.

There's a lovely woman in the nursing home, who has her car outside the home, at her disposal. She goes to mass in it regularly, goes shopping, sits in the car listening to the radio, reading the papers, waving at me when I come and go. She's a gem of a lady, always bright and cheery.

It brings me back to the time when first I was really depressed. I used to go shopping first thing in the morning, I would sit in the car with no agenda whatsoever, apart from facing into going home to the drudgery and routine of the day. I would look at people drive by, saying to myself; “they seem to have a life”, I wanted so much to be able to carry on with my working routine, be seen to be busy and employed. I felt useless, powerless, and impotent in the face of the reality. I was comatose with depression. I was also paranoid, afraid to meet any of my previous customers or friends, well, the few genuine ones I had. It was horrendously lonesome. The devil was beside me, urging me on to apocalypse.

I was at a rugby match in Lansdowne Road; it was Ireland versus France in the late seventies. I was in UCD at the time studying first arts. I was on the terrace, where I noticed a beautiful French woman standing alongside me, with her father. She had hardly any English, so I got a notebook out and wrote down what I wanted to say. She did likewise and it went on for 80 minutes, ending with a date for later that night in a nightclub in the city. We got on famously, total innocence, blind love, so beautiful, nothing else mattered at the time.

I kept in touch with her by letter and she invited me to her home in Paris that summer. I pencilled in June, as the Le Mans 24 hour race was held on that date and I wanted to see it, I would have the best of both worlds. I travelled by boat from Rosslare and on to Paris by train. I got to her apartment eventually and was met by her father and mother, who were most hospitable. The first thing her pa pa did was to bring me to the nearest café for a Guinness.

Roger was a detective superintendant for the Gendarme, he loved Ireland and rugby, and I was feted for a few days in Paris in summer. I was treated like a King, went around Paris in his Gendarme car on assignment, and out to lunch with his cohorts at work. Sylvie, his daughter, was one of the most stunningly good looking women I have ever met, she had it all. We visited art galleries, Momarte, had dinner with her friends, lounged around in bars and cafes, shopped in the clothes markets, had a ball. I didn't want to leave, but I had to get to Le Mans.

Le Mans for me was better than LSD; I had read everything on the drivers and teams partaking in the race. I may have well have been a passenger in Jacky Ickx's Porsche 936, a legendary driver back in the seventies who won the race numerous times. I camped at the circuit, where a whole village has been set up for the spectators. The Porsche club of North America is only a few metres away, guzzling down beers by a huge campfire, extolling their various driving exploits on their journey to Le Mans.

I am fascinated, I want to get into one of the Porsches and go for a drive around the circuit at breakneck speed. I am also there for the qualifying days before the race, as I'm obsessed with all the car constructors involved, the engine variants, the French opulence. I visit a few of the hospitality marquees and I'm invited into one, getting a glass of champagne, French bree, and decadent chocolate. I am at home here, this adrenaline fuelled carbon monoxide induced intoxication. I look at the cars passing in the blackness of the night and I see the glowing red heat of the turbochargers and brake discs on the cars as they pass at 300 kph. Jesus, I want to do this for a living.

I see a man around Killarney on his electric trike, with his two barking mad jack Russell's straining at their leashes to get on with it, keep on moving, it was a bit like me. I could never sit down for any length of time, I had to be active. This poor man can barely walk, but to watch him is inspiring, to see his determination and focus, its like Jacky Ickx going down the Mulsanne straight in Le Mans at 300 kph. The two dogs are better than the electric motor, such is their vigour to get on with it, and I wonder how their paws are from all the towing work. They are saying to him; "come on for fuck's sake, we haven't got all day". He is my "Ben - Hur" character.

I'm stuck in the middle of the Celtic Tiger madness, wondering what did I miss, where did I go wrong. I see ordinary people driving really exotic cars, cars that only the cognoscenti or professionals could aspire to years previously. BMW's, Audi 4 by 4's, Mercedes by the truck load. But when it comes down to the bottom line at work, it is the poor devil with the 10 year old fiesta or corolla that pays willingly, even offering a tip, unheard of when doing a fancy car; "you'll do better than that", being the retort when paying the bill. I'm wondering to myself how they can afford all of this madness.

A basic car wasn't good enough, firstly a brand new set of shining alloy wheels had to be obtained, inevitably leading to low profile tyres, discarding the perfectly good tyres on the car. Then, a sound system was installed with sub woofers and tweeters, amplification systems that would blow the ears off an elephant at 1000 metres. Of course the engine management system had to be re-mapped for more power, catalytic converters discarded for peak performance and a better exhaust note, and the intake system improved for maximum volumetric efficiency. Oh, I forgot to mention the speed limit was only 60 mph. I wondered to myself; "where the fuck are they going, speed week at Daytona beach."?

I feel inadequate in the face of all this madness, feel superficial, lost in a trance. What am I doing here? I'm listening to a discussion after dinner, the subject of property comes up; "oh, by the way, we had our house valued yesterday, 485,000 Euros, isn't that great"? I'm stuck for words; they may as well have been from mars, for all I cared. I used to get phone calls from an x- girlfriend enquiring as to; "what was I earning now"? I couldn't believe my ears. A regular topic that was regurgitated was skiing destinations in the winter. It was all bullshit to me; I would have been just as happy barrelling down the slopes sitting on a plastic fertiliser bag on a black run. I just wanted the adrenaline; everything else was only mindless drivel, a release from the dull Irish winter and monotony of the 9 to 5 workday.

I am at work on a January morning, its freezing cold, and work is slack. There's snow on the hills so I bring my ice axes and crampons to work, to sharpen them, point the crampons, edge the ice axes in anticipation of a cool adventure. The forecast for the following morning is perfect for the right conditions

I get up at 5 am; head off to the Reeks, my playground, in the hope of finding an icy gully somewhere. I always travel light, spare gloves, spare thermal vest, mars bar, bottle of water, though I eat snow along the way, its lovely when fresh. I'm on the second level, where there is access to a few gullies, my favourite being "The Lick," when frozen solid with ice and a light snow covering. I approach the chimney leading up to the start, without my crampons fitted; I can't stop as I'm fired up. It is treacherous, so I stop to don the crampons. It is also banked out with lots of snow, making it difficult to see the line of the climb. I attempt it once, and I am standing 5 metres up on 75 degrees of snow and ice, when my feet crunch through the ice, slipping back, with no protection. I back off, and on the third attempt I find the right line and reach the top of the crux. I'm elated, sweating profusely, looking back down at the steep ground with a great sense of achievement.

It's onwards and upwards to my own heaven, no stopping me now. I'm half way up the climb, where there's a small frozen waterfall of ice with a laid back approach, going on to a very steep step. I'm on the approach, digging in my crampons, ice axes stuck in; when suddenly a crampon comes undone, glides slowly back down the icy slope. I'm gutted, I can't move up or down on one crampon, so I cut steps across the ice, and slowly make my way across the flow, before carefully backtracking to retrieve my crampon, success at last, elation and escape all in a few minutes, though it seemed like time stood still. I reach the summit for the beautiful sunrise. Life doesn't get better than this.

I'm lying on the operating table after surgery, a pool of blood on my little pillow. I am knocked back to consciousness by a tapping sound to my skull, the surgeon wanted to break the good news to me; "we've got it out", the root of the brain tumour that is, at the second attempt. I don't know what to think, I'm very groggy but I can see a team of nurses and doctors looking busy as bees around the room. The pain is excruciating, but I try ignore it, I am delighted to hear the good news despite all the suffering. It's all positive from now on, ill just have to focus on recovery for the next year or so. Life is good.

John C is getting more dapper by the day at the nursing home, a new shirt and trousers every time I see him, a shining new pair of shoes. This man has a loving family, he is treasured, and he is a treasure trove of idiosyncratic sayings. Most people chose to ignore him, pass him by, but I don't, I want to engage with him as this is as good as it gets for him. I can appreciate that, I like it. He follows me into my mum's room numerous times, continuing the totally incomprehensible conversation. But I am interested, people smile at him, try to get rid of him, are embarrassed and stuck for words in the face of this unwanted visitor, but I never shrug him off. I would never slam the door in his face, unlike the bullies of this world, who would kick him out the door with no regard as to the consequences of their actions.

I often wonder why I invited bully boy into my sanctum. I had pity on him, he was obviously depressed for years on end, and he would appear at my door like a ghost, dishevelled looking, miserable, yet I respected him because he had very mediocre computer skills that I couldn't give a fuck about.

I always found better ways of using my time, mainly getting out on the bike or out on the mountains. Why was I so naive? I bent over backwards for this bollix, gave him work when his arse was out of his trousers, he had absolutely no self esteem, no empathy with anyone. Everyone was out to get him, so he treated everyone like a victim at his mercy.

I was always under pressure when he came at me, constantly telling me that I was no good, my equipment was shite, my laptop was rubbish, I was being robbed by my suppliers, I was a fucken idiot. I was always hypersensitive to criticism, especially with my work, and in this job that is the worst possible nature to have. I didn't have a thick neck, I took everything too personally and it got to me eventually. I felt inadequate in the face of all this character assassination, the constant knocking, and the despicable comments.

One day in January 05, there was a Swedish man missing on the hills. He had planned a walk from Kilgarvan via Mangerton Mountain and on to the Mcgillycuddy Reeks in very poor conditions. I went on that search for a couple of weeks and when it died down, when there was no sighting of him, I decided to go out myself , to look for his body. Work was quiet in January, yet one particular day, bully boy appeared at my door, scrounging around, sniffing out any bit of work. I told him it was quiet and that I intended going out at midday to search for the Swedish man on my own. He replied; "what did that fucker ever do for you, you think his family give a shit about you?" I just ignored him, went out on my own on the futile search, but in my subconscious mind, I was horrified by his thoughts and attitudes. I always just fobbed him off, that's the way he was. He had me over a barrel; I thought I needed him more than he needed me. He abused me at every opportunity, tormented me continually.

Suicide victims fail to see things coming, succumb to bullying, sexual abuse, torment, drug abuse, and reach a point of no return. There is no salvation in this world for them, they spontaneously and impulsively combust, the pain becomes so intolerable. Being the hypersensitive type is being open to extreme torment. If you are too smart at work or too good at your job, there's always someone ready and able to knock you on the head. Having an open heart is just as bad, as inevitably someone will try and take advantage of you, use you for their pleasure, dispose of you when you are no longer fashionable or cool, and move on to their next victim. Friends are like that too, when the shit hits the fan they disperse like a tornado, leaving you alone at its epicentre, facing expulsion, revulsion and annihilation.

Everything is fine and dandy when you are the life and soul of the party, people snigger at you as you just want to lose yourself for a brief moment, whether it is on a dance floor, in the pub, or wherever. Many of these people are too conservative to break out in a display of lovely madness or passion, but they take great pleasure in watching you make a fool of yourself.

I was always like that; I couldn't give a fuck about what people thought. I had too much of that shite going on with the in laws at home. They were so fucken uptight and snotty that they considered themselves superior to us, everything had to be seen under the glamorous spotlight, fashionistas my arse. They had this superiority complex and when they would come to our house, my poor mum was terrified, her back was up straight away, but being a total lady, she never once told them what she thought about them, yet when they left, she breathed a sigh of relief, and there was I in the middle, chomping at the bit and willing to strap a small device under their car in order to banish them for good. What is it about in-laws? Everybody has them, God help us and save us.

My poor brother lay on his death bed in CUH. He was in extraordinary pain, had organ failure and a blockage in his gut. He wanted it all to end, refused further medical intervention, he wanted out. Yet, along comes said in law, and decides to prolong the pain with further medical intervention, despite my brothers express wishes. The night before he died, we were called to his bedside, to say our final farewells; he knew his time was up. Poor mum was in a frightful state. We asked him about his funeral wishes, the mass readings, the hymns, and the celebrant. He made his wishes known, but when the in-law came into the room, it was like a nuclear holocaust, she dismissed every wish he had expressed from his death bed. I could have choked her there and then. Yet, nobody challenged her, it was the status quo in our house, keep your mouth shut, even when it was made known to us that we were not his family. How fucken degrading is that? A precursor to melt down for me!

I felt guilty enough about my own personal failures, but all these shenanigans multiplied the torment a thousand times. I always wanted to let loose with my tongue, but was unable to let my feelings known, thereby adding to my frustrations and guilt. Why the fuck did I come back to this country? I would have much preferred being in the outback of Australia, or in the Nevada desert building sand castles. What is it with people in this country? They pussy foot around, making shady deals with each other, smirking behind their backs at having pulled one over some poor bastard trying to make a living in an honest endeavour. The cute hoorism that was endemic, the lying and deceit all round us. I didn't want to live like this, I hated that environment, people building sand castles in the sky, boasting about their latest holiday destination, or their their shining new car, their 5 on sweet bathrooms, their walk in wardrobes, their ECT room? Ha ha.

After my brother's death, I'm cycling along the Eastern Cape, the wine country in South Africa. It is absolutely sublime; I am free at last from all of the shite going on around me. I don't want to get off the bike, the sun is shining, there is a beautiful warm breeze, and the scenery is stunning. This country was made for me! I feel instantly at home here, maybe my ancestors were cave men in Kwazulu-Natal?

I remember when working back in 1980 for Argo and their racing team, Nick used to joke about all the South African dictators and characters and he would be name dropping constantly, then we'd laugh it off. Names like Joshua Nkomo, Idi Amin, and Robert Mugabe, and of course Archbishop

Desmond Tutu. Yet, here I was , in this wonderful country, on my bike. I was in wonderland again. The country took my breath away, metaphorically and physically, as it was like I was on the Tour De South Africa, but on a mountain bike. Of course there was always the risk of violence hidden all around, the massive private security in place, security guards at the entrance to bars and restaurants, but I was happy here, free at last, free at last, no constraints on me.

We had a lovely guide, along with a young German kid who wanted to be a professional cyclist, Ben was his name, he was in transition year from school and got his dream job here, I would have killed for that opportunity, and I told him so. I tested him at every opportunity on the bike, especially when it came to steep climbs and hairy descents, and he revelled in the challenged, smiled with glee during the whole trip. We came in to Hermanus, on the Indian Ocean, a famous whale watching point where the whales migrate from the cold Antarctic waters to have their calves. We stopped at a viewing point, and I couldn't contain myself. I had to get in the water, so I swam out about 200 metres from shore to try and reach a whale and her calf, but they glided past me. This is as good as it gets.

There was a shady side to South Africa also, and you would want to be blind not to see that racism still existed and there were awful looking shanty towns on the outskirts of cities with no water or sanitation, but it was a terrible beauty.

I could have stayed there for months, it was invigorating. It was also at the time of the Rugby World Cup; when South Africa went on to beat England in the final. We watched many South African games in the pub, where we saw the extraordinary passion of the South African supporters, it was awesome.

Reality bit hard when I came back home. There was the constant grieving and the political tip toeing around the- in laws; I was on the road to perdition. I couldn't get away from the negativity around me, now coming at me from all sides. South Africa was a wonderful respite, but after being home for a few weeks, all the enjoyment was gone, my life was now teetering on a knife edge. I had no escape, I felt like a prisoner at home, and work was my only salvation, except for the small matter of the Bully boy. I had taken too many knocks over the years, and now I was on auto pilot, at the mercy of the computer, a crash was inevitable.

Wearing your heart on your sleeve is a recipe for disaster in this world. You give a lot, but the returns are minimal, you are viewed with suspicion, classed as a bit mad, opening your heart to all and sundry. I was never the cold calculating type, never over analysed myself or looked for an advantage over anyone. I was simple really, wanted to be loved and wasn't afraid to show it. I had a ferocious passion for the outdoors; there were no rules, no restraints, no dodging the bullet or character assassinations. Some people take pride at seeing you fall on your arse, both physically and metaphorically. They will have a great laugh at you behind your back, and come back for more. I would always be the first one to take on a challenge head first, with no regard for the consequences, I lived like that, it was more passion, it was invigorating, it was adrenaline producing.

I didn't care what people thought. Impulsivity is great; it is never dull or routine. It is a stupendous release from the banal. It need not involve expensive pursuits in far flung destinations; it is at your beck and call in an instant. My happiest days were spent on my bike, going on my own expeditions around Killarney, where on a summers day, I thought nothing of cycling around Muckross and Dinis, swimming the length of Muckross Lake, to the astonishment of passing boatmen, getting back on the bike to do the Gap Trip, have a stop for a pint in Kate's, sit out in the sun and watch the smelly traps go by in an instant. I wanted it to go on and on until I was physically spent. The music stopped when I reached home.

Johnny Cash had a total breakdown, as depicted in the well documented movie starring Joachim Phoenix and Reese Witherspoon. I think about that movie, the torment portrayed by his public meltdown, his addiction to drugs and alcohol. I can recognize first hand now, how he felt, how anyone felt in that hell hole that is inevitable for many people, most of whom never survive.

Johnny Cash was a musical icon when I was growing up, and it's only later in life that I appreciated the words in his songs, notably; "Folsom Prison Blues". It always touches a nerve with me when I hear it played. I may as well have been in prison alongside him. "When I was just a young boy, my mother said to me, son always be a good boy, never mess with guns, I shot a man in Reno, just to watch him die." That may as well have been me; pulling the trigger to wipe out the bully boy who tormented me for years. But I was no Johnny Cash, I didn't have the gun or the means to blow him away, I was too broken to even contemplate doing such a thing, I hated myself so much.

It's amazing to see ones perspectives change over time. Steve McQueen was another icon of mine, notably because of the infamous car chase in the movie Bullit. It didn't matter to me about plots and twists and rhetorical turns in the movie, I was just hooked by the muscle car, the burnouts, the driving through the streets of San Francisco. Nothing else mattered for me. He was the epitome of Cool. Yet, years later, I find out that he was a wife beater, a serial womaniser, a heavy drinker, a tormented soul who died young. All the more reason to admire him? Paradoxical, huh.

Sitting my leaving certificate English exam, I was asked to write an essay, outlining my imagination. That was easy, I picked Steve McQueen on his daring drive through the streets of San Francisco, of course my examiner didn't concur, I failed English, but who gave a fuck? I had fun for a fleeting moment of madness.

I'm on my bike, on the back road to puck, dreading bumping in to the bully boy. I think about lobbing a rock through the windscreen of his moving car, briefly. All the tension evaporates when I pass his hinterland. On my way back home, I consider cycling into an oncoming truck, ending my torment. That would be very messy though, not fair on the poor driver, not to mention the consequences of causing an accident. I make it home in one piece again, thank god. On other occasions, I think of the anonymous souls who took their own lives, by jumping in front of a moving train. Jesus, that sounds dreadful, poor devils.

I imagine the conversation the bully boy is having after my funeral; "Ah sure he was useless, couldn't do anything right, he couldn't make his mind up about anything".

My thoughts are inversely proportional to my moods at the time, but since the latest therapy consists of figuring out; "mind over mood", it alleviates lots of my torment. I have to change my thinking process, altering my moods. It is a very slow process, and I have to be incredibly disciplined in my own mind. That takes time, even though I have always been incredibly disciplined in my outdoor pursuits, it's just a follow on from that, though much more significant, equally rewarding and stimulating.

The self criticism is waning, slowly and surely day by day. I gain confidence from this new thinking, gain self esteem and self worth. I realise that I am a very lucky man, coming through all these traumas in my life. I'm on my own now, I have more time to discover my own mind, my own wishes, the new standards that apply to me, but I will have to be disciplined, very disciplined.

I take up Art and photography. At first, it is like going back to work, I am there looking at the finished article, looking for flaws, imperfections. I've taken some stunning photographs whilst out in the mountains in the big freeze, but I am never happy with them, I could always have taken a better one. But gradually I take a different attitude over time. I have to learn to stop this thinking and enjoy my work for what it is, for where it has led me. I'm never going to be Jack B Yates, but who cares; it's all in the beauty of beholder. Who cares if I don't sell any? This is my ongoing therapy, art therapy. I was never happy with my work anyhow over the years; I would consider myself a failure if I hadn't put back an engine better than it left the factory. Perfectionism doesn't work in this life, even though many try to attain it.

I always found it difficult to focus on one thought at a time. I had so many conflicting thoughts in my head, but they were all bright and wonderfully imaginative, they were never negative. It was only through contact with negative people that I was thrown to the wolves, I couldn't handle it. Every person has a breaking point and mine was at a higher threshold than most. My pain barrier was huge, having been through so many traumas in my life, so much pain and suffering both physically and mentally. I always wanted to please people, go with the flow, as I was unable to articulate my feelings, I was too shy.

As I was living at home, it was taken for granted that I would always be around, come what may, to be willing and able to help out. I was always frustrated living at home; I couldn't really invite anyone in as there were always callers to see my mum, mainly priests and nuns. I always felt like the little boy in the corner. Work was my sanctuary, my own escape from the torment of the real world. Once I opened my workshop door, I was in a different world, where I could express myself through my work. I took ferocious pride in my work, never did dodgy work, and was always too conscientious and honest. I took it all personally. I could simultaneously work on two cars side be side, my bi polar worked very effectively, I was always very clinical and methodical in my work. Of course I was a perfect target for the bully boy, he swooned on me like a vulture, and I was there for the taking, too naive and innocent.

Bi polar people are considered mad by most people, when in fact they can be highly intelligent once they can focus on a particular subject at a time. It's like having your brain divided in two, one side is just ticking over, getting on with the daily struggles, whist the other side is very expressive and creative, though it is not generally seen like that. Bi polar people can be very high achievers, and maintain impossibly high standards from themselves. They are also their own worst critic and enemy, as they constantly fail to reach those standards set by them. There are constantly conflicting thought going on in your head, feelings of guilt, low self esteem. One side is knocking the other, picking away at them, making it tormenting and disturbing. Add in a bully to the equation and you have impending disaster and self destruction.

I've been very lucky, I've lived on the high side for most of my life, had enormously rewarding experiences along the way. Many people with bi polar disorder are shunned by society, thereby locking themselves away in seclusion, seeing only the dark side of things, the depressing low side. I found routine life incredible boring and dull, hence my mad antics in cars and on the bike and up in the mountains. I had self expression in abundance, the sky was the limit, and it never failed me. It was my outlet, as I couldn't put into words what I felt; I had to experience things first hand. I was a huge risk taker, it was my bread and butter, and life was too dull otherwise.

I was driving to Dublin in '88 with my tool box in the car, all boxed for shipment to Perth in West Australia. I was undecided about going, but indecision was always a constant with me. I turned around numerous times and changed my mind, until after much turmoil, I eventually drove on up to the shipping company to send my tools on their way. Indecision ruled my life; I would never be able to make a hundred percent commitment to anything. Last minute.com should have been my calling card. It was like arriving at a junction at breakneck speed and not knowing whether I was going to turn left or right, whatever way the car was pointing, I would go with it.

But at work or out on the bike I was totally focussed. The impulsivity stuck with me when it came to marrying Karen, I just changed my mind at the last minute yet again, though after much soul searching. I was always thinking too far ahead, I didn't want to settle into suburban life in Canada, even though it was the natural playground for me, I found it very restrictive, too correct, and all my impulsivity would have to be thrown out the window. I didn't want that to happen. I couldn't function like that, even though she was the love of my life and I had gained an insight into what was to follow on, the road to perdition for me, subconsciously of course.

Karen had suffered her own turmoil ahead of me, but she had the skills to get through them, whilst I was thrown to the wolves to sort it out myself. I always had to gain experience the hard way, on the ground running. I had taken so many knocks, both physically and mentally, it couldn't go on indefinitely. Karen tried to tame me, to keep a lid on my exuberance and impulsiveness, even though she used to love it when I would call around unannounced while she was studying in Killarney. I would persuade her to drop everything and we would go off and cycle to Lord Brandon's cottage on a sunny day and enjoy each others company, laughing and joking along the way, stopping for a pint on the way back.

I always had to put a lid on those mad psychotic thoughts; they were always funny and invigorating. I couldn't stand boring nonchalant conversation for too long, I would move on; I had the attention span of a midge. Multi tasking is a synch for the bi polar person. It worked seamlessly, I could do 4 completely different activities in a short space of time and I would flourish at it, extremely satisfying. That's why I never wanted to work for anyone; it was too mundane, not stimulating enough. I wasn't built for that. I had the ultimate freedom in that I could finish a day's work by lunchtime, then head off on my bike or out on the mountains for a blast, it was divine. Sometimes I felt guilty about that and inevitably would rush back to work just to make an appearance, to show that I hadn't gone away. Sure who cared anyhow?

Concentrating on one topic in a conversation was very difficult, especially so if the subject was mundane or boring. If someone opened the door into my mind, I could extrapolate endlessly; I would have their full attention. That is why I fell in love with Karen; she was always passionate, spoke with intelligence, not the usual mindless drivel you hear from some so called adults, talking about their latest acquisition, their lovely new BMW with traction control, it just sounded cool, or their latest yoga holiday in Crete. It was all rubbish to me. I would have been much better off living in a place like Cuba, where you had nothing, had no aspirations about building castles in the air. Reminds me of that wonderful saying; "psychotics build castles in the air, neurotics live in them." That is why I survived; my own mind is a wonderland, endlessly uplifting, away from the banal and mindless routine.

I'm having a conversation in a pub with a drunk. I listen like a fool for too long, until my mind wanders into the endlessly funny ways that I could fob him off, get him to shut his trap, but I desist, I am too nice to break it bluntly, so I carry on the conversation, excruciating as it may be just to be sociable. My mind changes topics instantly, trying to cope with this endless onslaught of drivel, a relief valve if you like. Maybe I should have been put on a serotonin drip, or an adrenaline drip, and then perhaps I could have controlled my hugely energetic urges to get out in the air and release all those endorphins. I wasn't built for hanging around in the one place for too long, I had to hit the eject button on numerous occasions when I felt uncomfortable on social occasions, they were stifling me, too cosseted for my liking. I'm out of this kip!

Creativity is the cornerstone of the bi polar person, though they may not know it, to their detriment and ultimate expulsion from society. When I was in the psychiatric ward in Tralee, I was taken into a room where people were painting. I looked at it and said to myself; "sure I'm only a fucken mechanic, what do I know about painting"? The nurse tried to coax me to take a brush into my hand, but absolutely not, I couldn't even consider it, I was a total failure at everything I ever did, had no prospects, nothing to offer anyone, and my wrists were fucked anyhow, so what am I to do ? I'm surplus to society, even more so in this kip. I may as well end it all now, get it over with.

Now I love taking a brush to canvas, not knowing the outcome. But it is incredibly satisfying to look at the result the following morning. It might not be much, but you can release your imagination endlessly with the stroke of a brush, it doesn't have to be perfect, it doesn't matter if you can't sell it, it is the work of the soul and that is the ultimate gratification. Taking a picture is the same, incredibly rewarding to see the panorama in front of you, saying to you ; " yes, I was there, that was me ". As good as it gets.

Anxiety is a terrible emotion. I would be very anxious when it came to work. I was always anxious in case I wouldn't have done a perfect job. I would worry for a few days after doing a particularly difficult job, worried that the engine may drop a valve or some such thing. I didn't have a thick neck, and that was a big hindrance to me. It was the same out on the bike or in the mountains, if I didn't give it an honest effort, it was wasted. I would have to go out again later and repeat the trip in a better manner.

When scrambling on a route, I couldn't have gone around a particularly difficult outcrop; I would have to attack it head on. Nothing else would suffice. It was the same on the bike. Relentless progress in everything. I didn't realise how good it was, I just kept pushing and pushing myself all of the time, not realising what was causing my inner turmoil. I was on auto pilot all those years, trying to banish the mental pain in my life, the mistakes I had made along the way, the frustration of living at home and not having a partner, and blaming myself for the break up with Karen. It couldn't have gone on at such a rate; I was on the edge of a cliff.

People commit suicide because they feel they have nothing worthwhile to offer, they have no self worth, they are shunned by the rest of society and thrown to the mercy of the Psychiatric system. Lots of people give up after seeing their treatment in the various psychiatric units, the totally degrading behaviour, and the complete lack of compassion, the non stop drug therapy that deadens the mind, the cold treatment, the appalling conditions, and the forced ECT therapy.

When you are in that state of mind, this is the last straw as far as many people are concerned. It is the ultimate degradation of the person, soul destroying. Many people decide to pull the trigger, rather than be incarcerated at the discretion of the mental health services. Their lives have no further meaning, in this increasingly hostile world, and especially in recession times when many are faced with expulsion, from their work, from their mates, and from society in general. Sympathy is only a word.

Essentially, you are on your own at the end of the day, left to sort it out with yourself, painful as it may be, too painful for some, paying the ultimate sacrifice. I spent so many nights in bed wishing that I never woke up the following morning, it was unbearable. I had no outlet, no means of expression in any form, just existing from day to day, hoping I would drop dead somewhere along the way, comatose with grief and torment. I wasn't a worthy person, I punished myself more than anyone could ever administer. If there is a purgatory, I will have no need to go there; I have done my penance on this earth.

When you feel so unworthy about yourself, it is difficult to even consider a way through the mire, I felt it wasn't worth the effort; I had messed up so much along the way. The daily routine was mind numbing, no engagement with anyone, no meaning in my life, no one to hug you and offer a kind word or any reassurement, impending doom and gloom. People bypass you in the street, avoiding you at all costs, not wanting to associate with a depressive person, which was really hard. You were left alone and isolated; the only meaningful conversations were with psychologists and nurses, who tried to find the best drug combination to make you feel somewhat human again.

Nobody can understand what you are going through; you are scraping the bottom of the barrel, looking for any sign of hope or peace of mind, when in fact all you are doing is digging deeper into the abyss. Any gains are hard won, excruciatingly slow. You're reputation is shattered, shredded to pieces, ignominy and grief side by side. Your credibility is thrown out the window; as you cannot possible meet anyone's expectations in this state of mind, your family treat you like an invalid, uncooperative in any way, unable to conform to the status quo. You are viewed with suspicion by so called friends, who abandon you in your time of need, when really all you want is a kind word or a normal conversation, however brief.

Society has no time for people with any sort of mental health issues; you cannot be relied on to do any meaningful work, when the opposite was the case in my situation. I craved getting back into the work environment in order to ease my personal torment, but there weren't any jobs, nobody even considered that I was perfectly able to function at work; I missed the routine so much. Instead of going to work, I was forced into the job as carer when I was in no way prepared mentally for the job, even though I was caring for more than twenty years previously for both my father and now my mum.

Of course nobody came forward to offer me any work, despite being self employed for over 20 years. That was particularly galling and hurtful. The hard facts of reality hit home to me. You're on your own, you may as well be on the North Col on Everest in shorts and tee shirt as far as anyone cared, left on your own to the mercy of the elements, and ignored by fellow climbers on their way to the summit. Life can be ruthless.

Bi polar people need love too just like everyone else, but effectively you are ostracised from society at large, left to lounge around in self doubt and misery. I craved getting back in to a work environment; just a part time job would have suited. But the longer I stayed away, the more difficult it would be for me to get back to normality. In my case, I had too much time on my hands to think about where I was and how it came to this point. My mind was overactive at the best of times, but after recent events, it was running on empty and delusional, with paranoia and psychotic thoughts, constantly belittling myself and being self critical to a huge degree. Bi polar people need a focus or a goal to achieve, something creative or productive to be involved in.

Medication can be hit and miss, it's a fine art rarely perfected, but if incorrect can have devastating consequences both for the user and their families. You are at the mercy of the latest prescription in order to sleep and carry on the daily routine of life. Self destructive thoughts continued with me for a couple years, what with my already risky adrenaline fuelled trips on the bike and in the mountains, it was easy for me to drive on through the pain barrier physically torturing myself every time.

Taking anti depressants made me increasingly numb, unable to figure out for myself how to progress, I didn't want to be stunted, didn't need to be. I wanted to be alert and active, but not at the usual manic rate I had been used to. I had horrendous dreams and found sleep difficult. Peace of mind was non existent. I would continually fight the medication, the dosages, in the hope of eventually coming off them and finding my own peace of mind in my own way.

As far as I was concerned, my mind was not my own as long as I depended on anti- psychotic medication. I didn't know who I was, though I knew I had certain capabilities within me, gained from my previous exploits over the years, not always destructive tendencies. I hated being told how I felt, where I was and what I should do, how I looked. I hated being reminded of my associations with my previous working life, it was like being reminded of a false existence, pigeon holed yet again to my horror. Patronising never worked for me, I didn't like it. I was far better than that.

Bi-Polar from another angle has two very exotic parts from my perspective; The North Pole and The South Pole. I loved Tom Crean's epic endeavours in Antarctica all those years ago, his honesty, his demeanour, his totally unassuming character. If there ever was a role model for me ,well, here he stood; a powerful individual who let his heart do the talking, never shirked at a problem, the most noble and humble of people that ever grace this planet

The world seemed so small to me all those years ago, when I would look up at the destinations in Airports and see exotic names like Johannesburg, Mumbai,

Dubai, Santiago etc. Deserts and icescapes were something else in my book, really exotic locations, wilderness, which equated freedom, open spaces, no restrictions, I craved wilderness on a massive scale!

A work routine was my bedrock for most of my adult life, yet now I was expected to carry on as normal, be that same person I had been in my previous life, when nothing could have compared the two polarised existences. I had to blow conventional thinking out of the water. Value systems had to change, lifestyle changes had to be made, and I had to go back to basics, back to my cave. It was where I was happiest, no demands on me, no expectations, no false dawns. It was me and nature, trying not to be influenced by conventional wisdom or thoughts. It was up to me to find my own centre, that place where I could remain calm and content, appreciative of the little things again, not being taken for granted, not taking myself for granted.

I was no longer that same person in my previous life; I was much more considerate, more reflective, and more appreciative. Yet, I was still considered no different by people on the outside, and that put me out of kilter. My responses remained the same, but after a while, I lost interest because it felt like nothing had changed, for them maybe, but not for me, and they couldn't see the difference. It took me a while to cop on to it, but I persisted, I didn't want to be that same person they were talking to. If they couldn't see that change, then tough on them. It was their loss.

Moving on was extremely difficult, especially so when you are still in the same town, meeting the same people over and over. Your perception is that from the outside nothing has changed, but nothing could be further from the truth. Inside, you are trying to re-invent yourself, difficult at the best of times, impossible in my situation. I kept being reminded of my previous life, mainly my working life, and I didn't need to be reminded of my past.

When mum went into the nursing home, it was very traumatic for everyone. It was the last chance saloon, and she wasn't giving in to the final countdown. It should have marked a little relief for me, but no, I too felt guilty about sending her to a nursing home, where will it all end? This is when I learnt about art and art therapy. It was lovely to sit in a quiet room with no distractions, soft music in the background, painting away your sorrows, your pain. It was great therapy, though I found it very challenging but rewarding. You only get out of it what you put in, in simple terms.

I have been hill walking for 35 odd years, but never carried a camera, I was always rushing to get to the summit or get back for a pint after, too busy to stop and look around me, it was all a rolling experience and I had to feel the surge of adrenaline on the way. But I bought a small little digital camera and took hundreds of pictures over the last year or so and when I got them developed, they looked stunning, especially the snowy mountain pictures. I never bothered taking enormous efforts in setting up the camera, I just clicked briefly when conditions looked good, looked atmospheric. The end result was stunning.

Positive thinking was like a wet rag to me in my desperate condition, no amount of positive affirmation worked because I was at the bottom of a sewer. I could try it for a millisecond, but that was it, I was thrown back into the burner almost immediately, regurgitating all of those horrible negative influences in my life. It would take a couple of years before I could be happy in myself, my self esteem being rebuilt slowly but securely. I had to learn the trigger points that sent me into helter skelter, thereby avoiding those situations and also by avoiding negative influences which were all around me.

Chapter 6

Childhood Experiences

My father used to take us to Inchicullane in Kilcummin, where I had two uncles, John and Denis. They were small farmers, had a few acres and a horse called Dolly whom they used to pull a cart and plough the fields and so forth. They lived in this quaint old country cottage with no bathroom, a tiny kitchen and a parlour off the main living room, which consisted of a large concrete floor, a big table, a dresser for the "Ware", and a huge fireplace where a tree stump would be moved across to get every inch of heat from it. I never made it into the parlour; you had to be the Pope or John f Kennedy to gain access to the parlour. My father used to take us there on Sunday mornings usually, and especially so on Christmas mornings. We would be sitting there by the fire, literally in the fire, as you could sit by the fire and watch the plume of smoke going up the enormous chimney which went straight up.

Christmas morning was special, as the TV would be switched on at noon for the Urbi et Orbi blessing from the Pope at the Vatican. We would watch it quiet as a mouse, totally respectful and in awe of Rome and the throngs attending the ceremony. The conversation related to the comings and goings of the local characters nearby, the metropolis of Killarney, the price of stock, the price of drink and the talk of the young people gone mad with drink.

As my dad worked in the post office, he was seen as the man to go to in order to perform any kind of transactions or beaurocracy of any kind. Killarney may as well have been Las Vegas to these boys, as they had no car, but they had a lovely black high Nellie bike and I couldn't even get my leg over the bar on the bike it was so big. Excursions to town were rare, but they would go for a drink on Saturday nights to the Failte Hotel in College Street. A driver would be sourced for the expedition and they would regale tales they had heard on the night, wonderfully descriptive tones. These men were very humble beings; they didn't do extravagance or shows of any kind. They struggled to eke out an existence, to make the price of a few pints and a bit of bacon, but they did grow vegetables and spuds.

Denis in particular, was always bent over, he's spine was curved to a large degree and he must have suffered with the pain, but you never heard him complain. There were no visits to consultants in those days, no health insurance, you just put up with the pain and got on with it. Days were spend out in the fields, tending crops, setting or digging spuds, out to the bog cutting turf for the long cold winters. One particular day, we called in to the house only to see a huge pig suckling her young by the open fire; it was lovely, seemed so natural. No health and safety rules here. John was the man of the house as far as I could see; he was the delegator and had a great turn of phrase. I went up to dig some spuds one day, and was rewarded with a big fry up afterwards.

Denis was very adept with crosswords, especially those in the Sunday Press. He won many prizes, as the winners name was usually published the following Sunday. The Sunday newspapers were the highlight of the week for them, as they had a small radio and TV in the living room. The TV was rarely used as far as I could see. There were no distractions when visiting this house, all you could hear was the sound of timber crackling in the fire, the clock ticking away, and the odd conversation in between. We would look out the window to see if there was any car passing, but that was a rarity and they knew every driver passing. "So and so crashed into the yard last night, he was pissed as a Christian Brother", being one memorable sidebar.

Kilcummin was a great place, full of characters and stories. News spread like wildfire, and tongues were set wagging for days on end. The creamery was a focal point in those days, people congregated there and met their neighbours, chilled out for a while away from the toil of the day. The two boys were the ultimate bachelors, no time for women; too busy getting on with it, trying to live.

Going to the bog was a great experience for me. It involved driving down a dusty road and huge plumes of dust were thrown up in the air by the car as I looked out the rear window. It was like being driven down a tunnel of dust. I wanted more speed all the time in order to throw up even more dust, which was the highlight for me. It was all toil and sweat after that, but I loved the bottle of tea that we had brought with us and the bit of grub. The "Meitheal" syndrome was great, all working together with a common purpose.

My Aunty Mary would have been an actress; such were her comical antics in taking off people's fancy accents and their foibles. She too had a hard life, growing up in a farm in Crohane, outside Killarney. She didn't do subtlety, was straight up at all times, except when walking. She too had spinal curvature before it became fashionable. She was always bent over like my uncle Denis, and she would be drawing buckets of milk feeding the calves and other livestock in the farmyard at an awful rate.

My abiding memory of Crohane was when I was a young boy and I witnessed the killing of a pig out in the yard. He was strapped down on a table and his throat was cut, all the time squealing, which made me faint and have nightmares about for years after. The blood was drained into a bucket and was used to make black pudding later.

St Stephen's day was a monumental day in Crohane; it was like Christmas day all over again. Our family would be feted with a full Christmas dinner and whatever else you wanted.

The banter by Aunty Mary was supreme, she was a comedienne without knowing it, we laughed and laughed at her antics, it was like a different world. This would go on all day and into the night, eventually making our way home with belly's full and having been treated to a Cabaret show as well. It was iconic stuff, never to be repeated.

My Aunty Nora was a presentation nun for most of her life. She grew up in Crohane and when asked if she would join the Mercy Order, she declined, as she saw lots of discrimination and favouritism existed in their network, so she joined the presentation. The Mercy nuns were all over you like a rash if you happened to come from a well to do or professional family. If however, you were just a John or Jane Doo, you were sent to the back of the class, treated with contempt, and subjected to cruel jibes as well as punishment and humiliation.

Sr Nora started her convent life in Drogheda, where she kept in touch with many of her past pupils up until her death. She moved to New Orleans and then to Alabama where she spent much of her working life. Nora didn't do shy or covert, she was like Aunty Mary in lots of ways. I remember when I was in San Francisco in 1978, I decided on a whim to drive down to New Orleans to see Nora, but I underestimated the distance and I got bored with the endless freeways, so monotonous. The poor man who designed those freeways was definitely not a lateral thinker! Instead I took a left in Southern California after hours of freeway motoring and ended up driving across the Mojave Desert, the home of the Joshua tree. I loved that place.

I wasn't too far from Vegas, but I had no interest in that, I wanted the vastness and the freedom of the desert, the quietness, the beautiful cactus and rocks in the desert, the intense heat. I was at home here. Every now and then I would tune in the radio to the local station to get a handle on the people there and it was great. I saw lots of Derricks along the way, there must have been oil there.

It brings me back to my childhood when I was sitting in the great Dr Vass's chair getting some dental work done when he said to me; "There's money in oil, you should get into oil". How the fuck was I going to get into oil at 13 years of age? I was scared of my life at the dentists; before he got me to open my mouth I would ask him; what was that instrument for? and so on, until he lost the rag with me and sent me home happy, but I had no dental work done. I thought about oil for a millisecond and carried on regardless, he may as well have been from Mars.

The only oil I could get was a pint of Esso at the petrol station where I pumped gas for a few years. It was known as the Reeks Filling Station and I got up to all sorts of devilment there. On one occasion a Flanna Fail Rally was coming into town from the Tralee Road direction, so me and a buddy filled a can with petrol and waited across the road in Con Lyne's field before running across the road and dousing the petrol as the cortege approached slowly. As it came closer, I lit a match and watched a huge flame cross the road, before legging it up Con Lyne's field and watching in awe as the motorcade came to a halt, laughing my arse off at them.

The other favourite activity was driving around the petrol pumps trying to put a car up on two wheels on the way, we would see who could get up the highest for lap after lap of the pumps. It would be a customer's car left in for an oil change or a puncture repair and my favourite car was the little Riley Elf, a bit like the Mini, as it was impossible to roll it on to the roof, it was so nimble. It belonged to a nurse in the County Home next door and little did she know what her car was in for when she left it at our mercy. The other activity involved buying weed killer and sugar in the co-op in Killarney and making bombs and setting them off at the rear of the station. Spontaneous combustion was huge, with massive plumes of smoke hanging in the air for minutes afterwards.

One school friend of mine succeeded in turning a VW beetle onto its roof whilst mimicking my stunts around the petrol pumps, I had a great laugh for ages afterwards.

Motorbike mania was part of my life at this time. A great friend of mine from school, Anthony, was superb on a motocross bike. He had a Husquavarna 490, when he would often be seen going up the length of St Anne's Rd on the back wheel, pursued by a Garda squad car. Of course they had no chance of catching him, as he was a master on that bike, he could make it talk. I was not as good as Anthony on a bike, but he spent his days on various little bikes too, always revving the ass out of them, you could hear him for miles and miles.

I bought a Yamaha RD350 from a work mate and proceeded to break the sound barrier all over the place, god only knows how I survived. It ended briefly when I bent the conrods due to overevving, which necessitated me going to Dublin by train with the complete engine in a bag, in order to rebuild the motor at Mountjoy Motorcycles. This was the same leather bag that I used years later, to bag my tools at JFK airport, to the consternation of the check in girl. The bike was never the same again after that, I had run my luck, and reverted to 4 wheels again, my nine lives were on the countdown.

My Aunty Joan was one great character, she didn't do subtlety, came straight out with it, no pussy footing around. It made for great mental health, as she always said what was on her mind, no matter who was present, religious or otherwise. Anytime I met her over the years, I would come away laughing intensely after yet another diatribe of comedy or character assassination. She was pure gold. She was a Townie all her life, was street wise before it was the norm, and was a pleasure to meet at all times. She ran a B @ B for many years down New Street, The Orchard guest house, where she entertained all and sundry for years on end. She had a café in high street where I would be given a huge 99 cone on my way home from school on a regular basis.

O Meara's bar in high street was a regular meeting place in the early nineties. We would spend some of the best nights of our lives there. It was a pub with a small shop on the way in, which was run for years by two great characters, Kathleen and Donie, with the help of Joan, a poor woman who was in St Finan's mental hospital, and of course Smoky, the resident mongrel of a dog.

The greatest characters in town used to frequent O Meara's. It had a dart board in the small pub where we would spend lots of nights throwing at the board, inevitably missing the board after too much drink and hitting the ceiling on occasions. Any time you got a bag of taytos; Smoky sniffed them out and would come to get his fill, not leaving until the bag was discarded. Afterwards he would be sent to the "Hogan Stand", which was half way up the stairwell to the first floor. He knew automatically where to go as this was his exile from the pub when we had enough of him. He didn't have to be asked twice.

One St Patrick's weekend, we met an elderly American couple, Tom and Kathleen, and brought them to o Meara's. They didn't want to leave, and spent every night of their two week vacation in the pub. We joked that we would come over and see them and asked if it was ok if we could camp on their front lawn for a week or so. They never knew what to take as fact or fiction but they loved every minute of it. I convinced them that I was a sheep farmer, and i had come over the mountain from Kilgarvan with my stock. We were drinking from lovely Guinness pint glasses with a shamrock design for Patrick's day when they asked where they could get those glasses. I acted instantly and slipped out the back door with the two pint glasses under my jumper. As I stood in the laneway outside the pub, we were laughing profusely about it when suddenly the glasses crashed to the pavement, and there was Donie at the door of the pub witnessing the whole debacle, his eyes facing up to heaven, my eyes down to ground. I couldn't contain the laughing and neither could anyone else nearby. It was a gem of a pub.

Every night spent in O Meara's was a happy night. We may have gone to other pubs earlier in the night but we would always end up there. It was like a second home to us as you were always guaranteed entertainment no matter how daft it was. We were caught by the Guards one night for after hours drinking and were later summonsed and named and shamed in the Kerryrman newspaper, the ultimate indignity, and I had a fresh pint on the counter that I hadn't even taken a sip out of. There was a cold room in the bar and the running joke at the time was that Donal had gone to Lourdes with the ham to get it cured. It could have been the early 60's in Killarney; such was the atmosphere in the pub, definitely a time capsule.

O Meara's was a legion pub as regards club football was concerned. There were the Dr Crokes and the Legion clubs, both based in Killarney and they were polarised in every way. It's amazing to see to this day that certain people will not frequent a certain pub because it's a Legion pub or vica versa. We have the infamous Gooch playing with Dr Crokes and it must be very hard to support the Legion as they never seem to rise to the occasion, unlike Hugh Hefner. Rivalry was always intense, but as far as I've seen, there's no contest, the Crokes would drink you under the table, whilst the legion would be holding on to the table, picking up the scraps.

The country cousins were a great source of entertainment for us, as they seemed to live in their own cocoon. Apart from visiting my two uncles in Inchicullane on Christmas morning, we also stopped in to another Aunt, Hannah, from Deerpark just a couple of miles outside Killarney. This was a classic country house, as it was on a farm with all the accoutrements of the farm, mad barking dogs that would chase the car out of the yard and run down the road a few hundred metres after it, a welcoming committee if you like.

Hannah was a formidable woman, big and strong, didn't mince her words and was forthright in her manner, which didn't suit everyone. She was the "Solicitor" of the family, she ruled the roost. I remember, years later, whilst I was recuperating from my surgery in the 90's, she called to the house and unabashed, comes out with a classic; "show me your head."She wanted to see the scar on my skull, the sore shaved skull that had proved life threatening to me. Of course I was terribly embarrassed, and didn't turn my head around like a show pony.

I admired Hannah's toughness and forthrightness, if everyone spoke out straight and made their point, we wouldn't have all the subsequent illnesses that accompany that kind of mentality. I was brought up to be nice to everyone, if you were criticised or admonished in any way, you were to take it with a grain of salt. If anyone did anything nasty to you, just ignore it and carry on, laying the foundations of an increasingly fragile mental mind set. It lay the groundwork years later for my own susceptibility to bullying at work and my inability to speak out early enough and to criticise as warranted. I didn't know the boundaries as a result, and it was like the Mount Everest Syndrome; if you didn't get to the summit by a pre arranged time and schedule, then you were in danger of imminent death or near fatal injury. I never had that pre arranged time or schedule in my life, I went way beyond it and suffered the disastrous consequences.

Another destination on Christmas morning was to my Aunty Peggy's house in Ballagh. This house never seemed to have a light on, despite the dark and dreary days, but there was an old range where timber and turf would be loaded in to provide heat. Mick, the husband would be there pontificating about the impending Armageddon about to engulf the wide world, and also would go on ad- nauseum about the young people of the day, gone mad with drink and debauchery of all sorts, the speed of the traffic passing by the front door, the failure of our government and society at large. I nicknamed him; "The Doomsday Machine", and it stuck until modern times. One of his classic sayings was; "I pity the child in the cradle today." If you happened to be any way depressed, you would have gone out the back and ended it all in a brief frenzy of violence.

Aunty Peggy, poor soul, was a lovely creature, and she called my father out to the house one day to do her a favour. She pulled out a biscuit tin (USA assorted) from under the bed and he counted out around 12, 000 pounds or so, between post office savings certs and cash accumulated over yonks. She gave him the price of a pint on his way home for taking the trouble to sort this loot out and deposit it in a numbered Swiss account. The revenue commissioners are still searching for the bounty.

This was the same house that I passed at breakneck speed one day whilst testing out a Jenson Healy convertible, owned by an elderly hairdresser in Killarney. As she never passed 2000 rpm, the plugs would foul up regularly with unburnt petrol, so all it needed was to rev it into the redline in all gears and it would blow out all the carbon and drive like a mouse afterwards. Poor Mick would have had a heart attack if he'd seen me passing. I would pass he's house at around the ton, rev counter into the red, to get more and more speed out of the car, then stopping in Barraduff for an ice cream. The car was revelling in the moment, seemingly happy to have had a real master behind the wheel and begging for more. I figured a car like that was wasted in the dull pedestrian routine of its daily jog. Rev limiters were there to be used, powerful engines asked to be thrashed to the limits; they weren't designed for shopping mode, a terrible travesty.

Mad Lar was a local character in Killarney, fixated with rallying in old weapons of cars fitted with various exotic engines at the time, most famously, the lotus twin cam, fitted to a Ford Anglia or Escort. The story had it that a tourist was driving his lovely lotus élan around Kerry and he came a cropper on his dalliance, thereby the fancy lotus engine was acquired by the said Mad Lar and he proceeded to annihilate much more powerful cars at the time in various rallies. I used to call in to his decrepit workshop when he was building these weapons, and I was fixated by them.

I knew when he was going out for a test spin and I used to hear the sound of the car in the middle of the night up in Deerpark, where my Aunt Hannah lived. There was a circular route through the forestry land and I heard the missing beats of that twin cam engine from miles away, I was ecstatic. If my Aunty Hannah had caught him, she would have wrapped the crankshaft of that lotus engine around his neck! It was a route I frequented on my mountain bike 35 years later.

I was obsessed by speed as a kid; exotic cars in those days were few and far between. Only doctors and Lawyers owned a Jaguar or a Mercedes, the only real excitement came when the Circuit of Ireland rally came to Killarney. It was the climax of the year for me, this cavalcade of fast cars and the inevitable following of petrol heads from all over Europe. Legendary drivers like Roger Clark, Billy Coleman, Hannu Mikkola, the flying Finn Marku Alen, and of course the best of them all, the incomparable Ari Vatanen, who is now a member of the European Parliament.

My time was wasted going to school, I wanted to be a member of a Works Rally Team, yet here I was in that kip of a school, with Fr Dan Tit urging me on to join the Garda, when I would be sitting at the back of the class drawing various rally engines from a magazine, intoxicated with all the paraphernalia surrounding it. The mere sound of a high performance engine had me running out in the road to get the resonance in its wake. It was my drug of choice for years to come.

Of course, I really wanted to drive these cars, but I hadn't a hope in hell, the nearest I got was when my dad bought a brand new mark 1 escort and left me drive it on the day I passed my driving test at 18. By that time, I was a drifter, as they are now known. I took my fathers brand new escort for a spin down a forestry track, sideways to the hilt, before returning the car having cleaned all the murky evidence of my trip beforehand. The car was still crackling with heat for ten minutes after parking it. I thought the paint would melt, it got so hot.

Nothing else mattered to me at the time; everything else was only mundane and dull, sitting exams, being a good boy, trying to go with the flow, which was not my nature. I could only truly express myself whilst driving like a maniac, or otherwise cycling down rough forestry trails on an old bike, later to be developed into Mountain Biking. Being on the edge was my forte, no matter what discipline. I used to get an old bike and take the mudguards and carriers etc off it in order to lighten it and proceed to thrash it down the path beside torc waterfall and numerous other trails out around the national park.

I also played a little football, I made a great goalkeeper in the Monastery field, and I even trained with the Crokes for a while, but never seemed to get a game. So I took a transfer in the January deadline to the Spa club, where they promised to let me play, and they were true to their word, but I preferred individual sports, cycling, swimming or mountain running, not to mention driving. However, football was king in those days and there was no room for mavericks, I was on my own. When the leaving cert results came out, I was given four options; Join the priesthood, enrol with a teacher training college, join the garda or apply to the civil service. None appealed to me, I just wanted to take off into the sunset in a cloud of dust, free at last, free at last.

As most of my family went to Teacher training or further college, I was offered the chance to go to UCD. I had no idea about what I wanted to do, but it involved speed, the great outdoors, risk taking, rapid movement in every sphere. Imagine trying to explain that to a guidance counsellor in those heady days? Maybe a stuntman in Hollywood would have suited perfectly? It was right up my alley. However, I ended up in UCD studying first arts, history and economics. Talk about a fish out of water, but I loved being away from the constraints of home.

Between lectures, I would be engrossed in Autosport magazine or Motoring News reading the latest rally reports from the world over. Talk about a one track mind, I wanted nothing else only to be involved in some way with a professional race or rally team, yet here I was in a totally alien environment, out of my depth, but I was only passing the time, enjoying my freedom. I even wrote a letter to Enzo Ferrari asking if I could drive the latest supercar that came out of the factory. Of course I never got a reply, but a dumb priest never got a parish.

As I had no hands-on experience with cars, then how could I possibly get involved in motorsport in any capacity? Eventually, after one year in college, I started an apprenticeship in Killarney Autos. I figured that if I wanted to get involved in motorsport in any way, then firstly I would have to serve my time and do it the hard way. Those were the days when austerity was the norm for most families; it was a grind for parents with large families to feed and clothe them as well as educate them.

I figured myself as the black sheep of the family, not having completed college when everybody else seemed to aspire towards a degree or a professional qualification. Yet, I was in no way academic, had no interest in further education, I just wanted more driving experience in powerful cars, wanted to work on my car control skills and to learn about cars. If any fancy car came in to the workshop, I would try my best to get a road test in it, finding the limits of adhesion and passing them frequently.

I spent the first year in Cork, at the ANCO training centre, where we were thought welding and metal work and all the sundry activities involved in car repair and maintenance. I stayed in digs in Douglas, where the landlady was an alcoholic and when we would come in for dinner in the evenings, we would find her swigging a bottle of whiskey and falling out of the chair, no food on the table, no prospect of dinner. We had to resort to plan B, and get out of there fast.

I used to go home most weekends, sometimes hitching a lift, but on one memorable occasion, a buddy doing a painting apprenticeship was doing a job for an old lady and in payment she said he could have the Ford Anglia outside the front door for a fiver. This Anglia had a boot that wouldn't open due to crash damage and it also had four slick tyres, which made for interesting driving. We just made it to Ballyvourney by the grace of god, when fuel was getting low, so I pulled over and put 50 pence worth of petrol in the tank, where access was by opening the trunk and filling away. By Killarney, the poor Anglia was ready to expire, so I abandoned it and walked away, it had run its last race.

I sometimes stayed the weekends in Cork, especially when the Cork 20 rally was held. I would hitch my way around the countryside in order to see some of the stages, and one year in particular, Ari Vatanen came to Cork whilst in his prime, and he was a superstar even then, driving the lovely Black Beauty Ford Escort BDA. The man was a genius behind the wheel; he could make that car talk. He would approach junctions at an impossible speed, yet a brief dab on the brake pedal and he was gone in a cloud of rubber smoke. He was in a different driving league to everyone else, had more balls than most, some of whom had the same equipment more or less, but proceeded to embarrass themselves by losing it at the final approach or sliding too wide on the exit of a bend.

Billy Coleman was the Irish equivalent, but even he seemed to be minutes behind Vatanan when the resulting stage times were published. A certain David Sutton built Vatanen's cars, whose Alladins cave of a workshop I came across in North London years later, Of course, I wanted to be Ari.

February was usually a cold bleak month, but every year without fail, I made it to Galway by hook or by crook, to see the Galway International Rally. It was a magical place in the late seventies early eighties, I loved going to Galway, great atmosphere, great buzz, exotic drivers from Factory Teams who would use this event as a testing ground before the infamous 5 day Circuit Of Ireland Rally.

I had organized an interview with the Rothmans Rally Team director in the bus station in Galway, as that was where their cars were based. They had a huge profile back then and ran 3 Porsche Carrera's at the time, one for Billy Coleman, one for Qatari driver Saaid AL Haijri, and for the Circuit Of Ireland they ran one Henri Toivenen, a hugely talented driver who lost his life in '86 when his car, a Lancia Delta, burst into flames after hitting a tree on the Tour De Corse. I went to meet the sporting director in the freezing cold bus station and he asked me whether I had any previous experience at this level. Of course I knew then that I had little chance of getting work as I had practically zero experience at that level, but I was an avid enthusiast. I never heard back from him, but I kept my hopes up.

There was something magical about Galway in those times, the Great Southern Hotel was the base for the event and the craic was mighty there. All the rally bulletins would be sent around giving updates on driver's stage times and drivers who had retired. It was the perfect testing ground for the factory teams looking to gain experience on tarmac and getting the car settings right for bigger events ahead.

The highlight for me was when I went to the scrutiny just a couple of miles from the city and I spotted this lovely Porsche Carrera RSR, an incredibly powerful machine, and I asked the driver if he would give me a lift into the city. He duly obliged, and I was in ecstasy when I heard the roar from the rear engined racing flat 6 motor. It was a dream car of mine, and I never forgot about that short little spin. I still remember the cars registration number; CMR 911, driven by John Tansey. After that experience, sitting into any run of the mill car was very dull. I hitched around Galway to see the stages and it worked very well, as I saw more stages than lots of people who seemed to be driving non stop to gain the best vantage points.

Normal work resumed after these fabulous weekends, until the next rally, which was the West Cork rally and so on. My life was totally absorbed by getting to good locations on various stages and watching the outside adrenaline passing me in a fleeting moment. The Circuit of Ireland in its old 5 day format was my favourite rally. I must have spent more early mornings on Molls Gap than anywhere else. Killarney was the base for this event for years, and the atmosphere was electric. Drivers like Paddy Hopkirk in the early seventies in his diminutive little giant killing mini and onwards to jimmy McRae, Russell Brookes, the list went on and on.

Rally followers in those days were well heeled, mainly Brits, and they drove beautiful cars like the Lotus Cortina, the Twin Cam escort as well as lots of minis. The spectators drove an assortment of fancy cars including a few Rolls Royce's. They were far removed from the latter day rally followers, who seemed more interested in doing doughnuts in the middle of the road, ad nauseum. At least, I worked on my car control skills endlessly, there always had to be obstacles along the way, usually down forestry tracks late at night, I loved loose surfaces. Ultimately, I was living in dreamland, as I had no means of getting into a situation where I could get a drive; I was too gung ho, lived by the seat of my pants, though I never gave up the dream.

I navigated for a driver for a few rallies, but I wanted to be the one behind the wheel. It was the same story when I worked for Argo in Norfolk; I wanted to drive the cars in the test sessions, especially those beautifully sounding Formula Atlantic single seaters. I envied the drivers coming to the factory for a seat fitting, once the cars were built and ready to go. A plastic bag would be filled with a fast hardening compound and placed in the car; the driver would sit in the tub thereby moulding the perfect anatomical seat. The drivers would transfer these seats to the spare car if there was a hitch along the way.

I loved the cosmopolitan nature of the sport, drivers from Brazil, the US, not to mention the European drivers. The most laid back drivers were of course from South America, they were really cool and chilled, and they usually had beautiful women accompanying them on the pit road, of course I loved to see them, they added colour and vigour to the whole macho business of racing.

During my training in ANCO, I wanted to be a Formula 1 mechanic, to be on the front line of developments alongside my boyhood heroes, Jacques Villeneuve, Nikki Lauda amongst others. As time went by however, things didn't work out that way. The training at the time was more in line with doing the basics on mundane boring road cars, how was I to learn about racing and rally cars if I didn't get the proper training?

A racing mechanic at that time had to be primarily an expert in fabrication and welding of all sorts, mechanical work was in no way comparable to what I needed to learn.. Usually, a team bought in the engines and transmissions from specialist suppliers and if there was a problem with an engine, then it would be taken out of the car and sent back to the factory for a post mortem, before returning a fresh one to the car. I was to learn this years later whilst working for Argo, and the rally teams operated the same way.

I read technical books for years and years about construction techniques, engine building, turbocharger installation and plumbing and so on in order to keep up with international developments, but I was stuck at the bottom end of the ladder doing monotonous work on crap cars as far as I was concerned.

NASCAR racing intrigued me for years, especially the Daytona 500, which takes place in February. This track had a 45 degree banking and the cars would lap the circuit at 200mph bumper to bumper, until the inevitable side swipe would send the whole lot into a frenzy of avoidance action, culminating in a huge chain reaction crash whereby the drivers would invariably crawl out under the wreck to spontaneous applause of the 200,000 or so watching the race. Even the names of the drivers said something about the sport, names like Dale Earnhardt or Ironhead as he was affectionately known as and who lost his life at the Daytona 500 in a seemingly minor crash, or the infamous Richard Petty with his life long sponsor STP oil, a legend of Nascar, it was all the same to me, speed was the ingredient I craved no matter what the discipline.

However, life doesn't always go according to plan, especially so since I never had a plan, I just wanted to be involved in some capacity with motorsport. Everything else I did just happened to fit in, the cycling, the mountaineering, equally rewarding pursuits. I had no plan B, you take what you can get and move on.

All my life I had conflicting thoughts, contradicting me at every move. My thoughts worked like a pin ball machine, just pull the lever and the subject would change endlessly, very entertaining but hard to understand for most normal people, it was the same whilst at work, I could always have been doing something more spectacular, more invigorating, rather than be stuck under the bonnet of some mundane car. Mountaineering was the same; there was always another peak over there somewhere, a particularly challenging gully thrown in to make it interesting. Out on the bike, the same again, that route could have been better.

It is difficult trying to explain bi-polar to a normal person, it's all great crack when the subject matter is entertaining, but it is impossible to look into the murky side, as you are trying to keep that compartment secret and away in its own world. I always had a much more serious side which I entered into freely in my relationship with Karen, but after that relationship petered out, I had no means of expression in that same mode of thinking.

Everything afterwards was only an aversion tactic to make it seem that all was well and I was back to my previous self, but nothing could be further from the truth, I was pining for that same intellectual intimacy, for some equally understanding soul to come along and re-open that lovely compartment in my mind that lay dormant for far too long. It was my own Holy Grail, all of those precious moments where we would spend quiet times in each others company, pontificating about life, relationships needs and wants, with no interruptions in the way, no distracting thoughts or influences.

Of course it was only one part of my mind, but the most rewarding segment by far, even comparing it to the many manic exploits out in the great outdoors. Psychoanalysis for me was incredibly painful at first. I rebelled at the thought of it, especially having seen someone I loved involved in that practice for years, and who I helped along her tortured way to redemption, however daft it may seem. I thought I had all the angles covered after that particular relationship but little did I know of the impending breakdown it was to cause me personally years later.

I wanted so much to be valued for whom I was, to be recognised for what I was, but never again found that someone special who could walk with me side by side as my soul mate. That hit me really hard when reality dawned on me; I was like that polar bear out in the ice flow with no prospect of food or nourishment of any kind, no one to take my hand. From that moment on, I was all alone. I never moved on from that relationship, the torment it produced in my soul was devastating, yet I was trying to carry on as best I could in the face of my inner demons.

I tried self diagnosis before the shit hit the fan, but all I came up with was extremes of all sorts and I could see myself in all of those various psychotic scenarios and mentally disturbing images. I couldn't distinguish the facts from the reality, but realistically, my fate was sealed. If I was going down that road, then it was never ending and negative to say the least.

I was suffering from so many different ailments that I couldn't distinguish which was the uppermost priority illness. Everything from post traumatic stress to manic depression and the various spectrum disorders came into the equation, not to mention the bullying that went on, where the fuck do I start? Each particular diagnosis was extreme in my own mind, I had to be the worst ever, nobody could have suffered like I had, having a plethora of traumatic mental illnesses that could in no way be treated by any psychologist, ever.

I thought back to my childhood accident when I was hit by a car when only 5 years old. I ran down Hilliard's lane and onto High Street into the path of an oncoming car, suffered a fractured skull. I investigated pre-frontal cortex brain injuries and I discovered that many soldiers involved in conflict had serious injuries in that area of the head and it led to lesions in the brain in the pre-frontal cortex area, causing uncontrolled rage, personality changes and various emotional problems, manic depression amongst them and of course post traumatic stress.

Bingo, said I, that must be the problem! Jesus lads! That was hit on the head by my psychologist when he asked me was their any evidence of brain injury after my accident. Of course I hadn't, but in those days the only thing my consultant was concerned about were my motor functions and the physical healing process. If he only knew about my later motor functions!

I loved collecting Corgi Cars during my childhood, and I wasn't happy until I inflicted damage on them and creating a mock accident scene. Now there was a good reason for a psychiatrist's intervention, to stem the flow of what was to follow. Little did I know, years later, I would be involved in several near misses and life threatening accidents. It was the same story when I bought a new mountain bike later in life, I would have to thrash it down some muddy single track in the National Park just to make it look like a work horse. It was telling me that it was put through its paces rigorously, and survived to tell the tale, in all its muddy splendour. It had to work hard for a living with me.

I was always a bit of a loner, enjoyed my own company, loved walking for hours on end, getting lost in the mountains was so invigorating, so challenging, so rewarding to walk back from the unknown ground to familiar territory, a great sense of achievement to arrive exhausted back to have a pint in some remote outback and have a chin wag with a sheep farmer about how great a day it had been. I would saunter on home happy in the knowledge that I had survived another epic, known only to me, it was my world.

I was never a team player, which is why I never liked to go on expeditions to the greater ranges. It was painful to listen to all the talk and bullshit that existed in these circles, motivational speaking crap and all of that. I didn't need that shite, I just wanted to get on with it and make the summit in one piece and if not, so what, I would survive on my own, and that's how it went, until I came unstuck.

I needed help but I couldn't ask anyone. I'd have preferred to end it all, quietly and subdued, in some remote outback in those lovely mountains. No more endless team meetings, psychologist's reports, counselling, drug therapies, ongoing humiliation personally for one who had been so intellectually intimate with one woman ever in my life, not to mention physically. I was that other Canadian goose for fuck's sake, and I flew away.

I was a bit like Groucho Marks; I didn't want to be a member of any club who would have me! I preferred doing things my own way, even though it was paved with imminent danger and risks along the way, but sure that's how life is supposed to be lived. Structure was not one of my favourite things, organisation either, if there was too much forward planning involved in anything, then it took the element of surprise away, it became monotonous and dull. No reconnaissance of any sort for me, I would blaze a fresh trail through the snow for others to follow, at their peril. That is why I couldn't get married, there was too much predictability about it, and it was too planned, too structured for me.

Anyhow, what's the chance of meeting like minded women when you are bi polar? The Hadron Collider has a better chance of finding the infamous black hole particle under those beautiful Swiss mountains. As bi polar minds have infinitely variable chemical imbalances, you have as good a chance of meeting your soul mate in a game of Russian roulette, now there's a trigger point! Maybe if Stephen Hawking was the matchmaker at the annual Lisdoovarna shindig had I any chance of meeting someone remotely like minded!

Carl Jung once (or maybe twice) said that the root of all mental illness is sexual frustration, and that is like kerrygold, its pure true. When you are in a relationship, everything is fine and dandy, until the shit hits the fan, then the complications begins, you want to get out of the relationship for whatever reason, but it is very difficult to move on. This is when the self doubt begins, and if you keep going down that road, it is never ending, torment, guilt, disappointment, frustration, regrets.

In the back of my mind, I always wanted to marry an American woman or a foreigner of some persuasion. There was something too calculated and clinical about Irish women. They lacked spontaneity, passion, were too mindful and conservative. You had to meet all these ridiculous unspecified criteria, they were so insecure in themselves, never seemed to let themselves go, afraid to go mad for a night of sex and passion, unless of course copious amounts of alcohol were involved. In that case, the following morning, they would be scratching their heads wondering "What the fuck was I doing with that Oinseach"? Of course if you had a house and a fancy income and a pensionable job, they would swarm over "A good catch". I never liked fishing!

This brings to mind my sojourn in Boston in the late seventies after meeting this lovely American woman in Cork. She was smitten when I told her of my trip over the County Bounds in the snow; it was as though I had come up to the Second Step on Everest, sidestepping bodies along the way, she was really impressed with it. We got on famously and as a result I was invited over to Boston for Christmas.

It was my first time in the USA and I was seriously impressed, especially so by the dude in the black Cadillac, one of her friends, rather more so by the Cadillac, the huge bench seat where you could fit a small family with ease, the lovely purring sound of that V8 motor, music to my ears. I couldn't get over the electric seats and windows, where by the push of a button, in an instant, your command was obeyed, just like a rocket launcher. It was only when I met her sister that I was really eager to get to know her and the tension in the house was palpable; I was getting incredulous looks from my so called girlfriend of the moment.

Eventually Patty got pissed off with my lack of interest in her and my eagerness to get to know her sister, culminating in the offer to accompany her on the ill conceived road trip to Florida in the Transam that never materialised. I was totally overwhelmed with my reception at her Boston home at first, there was a party atmosphere in the house with all and sundry present, the hospitality shown to me was previously unknown, and their enthusiasm to meet a real Irishman was infectious.

There was only one problem; I couldn't relate to them on that same level of communication due to my shyness and I tried to avoid the spotlight, but it was impossible. I made do with the excuse of tiredness and jetlag, not to mention unfamiliarity with these new friends that suddenly appeared out of the bushes. They were confused, to say the least, and wondered whether I had a tongue; well, I had, and I would have preferred to use it down the throat of her lovely sister, but nothing was forthcoming.

I had a contact in Boston at the time, a retired policeman whom I met on a few occasions. It was pre arranged before my arrival that he would pick me up in Logan airport, but when I arrived at the airport, I was told he had gone to Florida for some super bowl game. Dan was a police officer in Boston for most of his life; he had emigrated from Ireland as a teenager and got a job with the police in Boston. He was now retired and in his seventies, but was full of vigour and life.

On our first meeting, he picked me up in his lovely white Cadillac, extolling the virtues of its anti- skid technology on our journey to the notorious Paul Reveres, a lap dancing club in Boston. Dan seemed to have no inhibitions about declaring openly to my friends as to where he was taking me, and when we sat at the bar these beautiful women danced on the bar in front of us, it was so close that you were almost intimate with their private parts, to my astonishment, but to Dan's delight and pleasure. It was ok to look, he said. I was enjoying the show too, though unsure of what my responses should be in this context.

My girlfriend Patty laughed at the thought of it and they seemed to view Dan as a little different from the norm, a bit eccentric, but I wasn't complaining, every trip with Dan was exciting and new. He brought me down to the police academy and showed me around, even the equine unit where the police horses were groomed to perfection.

We went up to New Hampshire for a weekends skiing, and stayed in a lovely log cabin near Cannon Mountain, where I witnessed the American Dream in action. Cool people pulled up alongside us in their lovely Corvette Stingray's and fancy four by four rigs with their skis strapped on to the roof, and their model girlfriends alongside them, looking as if they came out of a Vogue magazine spread. I felt a little intimidated by all of this, I wanted to be driving that Corvette, and be an Olympic level skier showing off my bravado on those icy slopes, instead of falling on my arse and crashing into every tree in sight on my way down to the Après Ski.

Roll on about 33 years and I'm in San Anton, that lovely chic ski resort in Switzerland. I decide to get lessons for the first few mornings and in the group was this lovely mad Russian nurse who worked on an off- shore oil rig, and as she smoothly descended the slopes, we laughed at her caution, her antics along the way. We met them afterwards at the Après Ski, downing copious amounts of gluvine and recalling the near misses of the day. Her friend had gone snowboarding and she appeared to have purchased her stupendous Tommy Hilfiger ski wear on the first morning. They had silk gloves for the Après ski and took a couple of days off for some serious retail therapy in the very expensive shops in the town.

During one morning session, I kept pushing the instructor to get him to move out of my way, he was too slow, and I barrelled past him to keep the momentum going. After those few days, I ventured off with a few buddies into off- piste territory; bad mistake. I ended up with a torn calf muscle amongst other muscular leg injuries, but I skied back down to the bottom station and once I discarded the skis, I found it painful to walk, but it's our last day so I'm not too concerned. Walking through the airport terminal was torture, and when I got home, it took a few sessions of physio to get back to reasonable fitness levels. But once I got on a mountain again, I ran myself into the ground with my legs not fully recovered, I thought I was invincible.

I made lots of pen pals in my early years, mostly women, in fact all women. One was Licia from Chattanooga in Tennessee. I never met her, but she sent me a photo of her and her family in their living room. She was gorgeous, and she shared tails of the local bike gang warfare going on there at the time. I was absorbed by all of this and wished I could be part of the gang, it was exciting stuff. She wanted me to come over, but of course it never materialised, but the thought of it was nice, especially from the inviting pose she struck from that lovely photo by their mantle piece. Maybe it was because I felt safer at a distance; I could control things in my correspondence, when I wouldn't have been able for the overt scrutiny and exposure on that personal level, I didn't have it that way, but I was a rogue, I didn't want that kind of confrontation. I wanted to run with the wolves.

Another pen pal of mine was that lovely Japanese girl, Takako, whom I met in Perth. She gave me her contact details and duly wrote to me for years afterwards. She even came over to Killarney to see me whilst holidaying in Ireland, and she looked great. She was very impressed with Ireland and the property boom here, and the size of the houses in particular, as Japanese homes were the size of a garden shed, especially in the cities. She invited me over to Tokyo but I never made it there. Jesus lads, I was spoiled for choice; they were dropping in front of me!

Takako stayed in the old Park Place hotel in Killarney. She phoned me out of the blue one day and I met her in that lovely hotel one evening. We had a great chat and she visited my mum at home and was really impressed with our neighbourhood and she couldn't get over the fact that we had a garden at the front and also at the rear of the house. She said that in Japan they would build around 100 apartments in that space. Maybe I should have been a developer?

During my time with Karen, she often mentioned my previous girlfriends and whether I was still in contact with them. I detected a little jealousy and wondered to myself whether I should find a local woman instead of going through all this torment with Karen just to get a bleedin marriage certificate. There was my gorgeous neighbour Claire, a stunning looking teacher who I got on great with and when she came to my door one night to ask me for something or other, I wondered to myself whether I would be a lot better off marrying her as she lived only a few doors down and had a good job and was very attractive. I wouldn't have the same microscopic scrutiny of my inner psyche, or the tormenting paperwork involved in the emigration process.

Then there was Angela, a girl who I met in Doheny and Nesbitt's pub in Dublin in the early eighties when I just came back from England. I was out of my tree with drink when I spotted her sitting at the bar with her friend. We got together and for about 10 years or more, we stayed together, more or less.

Trouble was, she was never happy with what she had, even though she had a teaching job, that nice little earner where she could have retired into the sunset with the infamous Croke Park Agreement pension package, much maligned by the private sector. She had much higher ambitions and went on to the Bar, having studied law in Blackhall Place. Whilst there, she made contact with various builders and developers eventually becoming a developer herself with a huge portfolio of property all over the country. All I ever wanted was that little country cottage like my uncles John and Denis, with a little garage on the side with its own rolling road and wind tunnel, not to mention an engine dyno!

Angela had a good heart, but was never happy with me being a humble mechanic, she wanted me to be an engineer or gain a professional qualification, but I just wanted to mess with cars, full stop. Maybe it would have made interesting dinner conversation; "oh, by the way, my husband is an engineer, he just designed the Four Seasons hotel," instead of; "Jeysus, my fella's breaking his bollix trying to line up a clutch out the back in the dark with just a head torch for light, will you go out and tell him the Flintstones are on TV and the kettles on", Yabba daba do! One mans meat is another mans poison, I was happy with the latter.

It all came to a crashing end for Angela and her property empire, as it did for numerous developers, thereby setting in motion the savage austerity plans set in place by the infamous Troika in order to pay the piper.

I felt inadequate in the face of all this property speculation, the acquisition of assets, empire building. I was just as happy in my own cocoon, car therapy. I couldn't give a fuck about gaining wealth or anything like that, I just lived for the next adrenaline rush up a mountain or on the bike, it was my escape. It was only when I got back home that the music stopped, reality hit hard.

I know now what cyclists mean when they take a rest day in the Tour De France, where they get on the bike for several hours just to keep turning the legs, its as if they are afraid to stop for a day as there's too much time to kill hanging around in their hotel, too much time to think and analyse themselves. I lived like that for years, I was afraid to miss a day out in the mountains as I didn't want to lose all that fitness I had built up over time, I needed to keep the momentum going, even though I was no professional sportsman. It was all I had, as my business was just a means to go away on all these adventures and live the dream. I wanted it to go on forever.

So the party ended and life sucked, the reality of still living at home, with my mum depending on me again after all the opportunities I had left behind, that really rankled with me.

On the bright side, I had survived total meltdown, barely. I was still at home, though now on my own, except for the fact that it was open house to other family members who deemed it to be their holiday home whilst I was left to clean up after their too frequent visits. "It's the family home", was the regular retort to my frequent objections to their intrusions, and especially so to one brother in particular, who was the bane of my life since childhood, Tim.

Bad blood would be a mild way in describing my relationship with Tim. We never saw eye to eye, ever. I suppose it goes back to my childhood days when Tim was a bit of an academic at school whereas I was a nerd, only interested in getting out at the break and running around playing any sport I could, getting up to any devilment along the way. I shared a room with Tim for too many years and he loved to read and read and read into the small hours. I couldn't sleep with the light on; so on one particular night I got so fed up with it that I took the bulb out of the socket and an altercation developed. I belted him in the mouth, bloodying his face and causing uproar in the house, I was a quiet boy afterwards, for a while. This was a recurring theme in my life, I hated being near him.

Roll on twenty years or so and who ends up driving me to Cork CUH with my brain tumour? I was getting sick in the car constantly and on top of this I had to listen to Tim talking non stop some drivel about it being Gods will or something to that effect, it was bad enough to concentrate on just making the journey but this torment on top of it took the biscuit. I just wanted to get to bed to lie down and die in peace if it was Gods will. If it was god's will, then there would have been an ejector seat in the car!

Coming around after surgery, I woke up briefly in excruciating pain to the sight of Tim sitting in the chair by the bed. I pretended to be asleep rather than listen to his absolution and numerous other religious sidebars. Eight hours rolled on and I opened my eyes to see him there still, I can't believe it, my pain is multiplied by ten, emotional and physical. What do I have to do to get rid of him? I can't even wallow in my own pain and try and get some piece to get on with my recuperation.

Tim was the consummate civil servant; if you wanted to make a mould of a civil servant, then here he was, polished and buffed by years of beaurocracy and public service. Chalk and cheese come to mind! We couldn't have been more different.

One Christmas morning I gave him a chemistry set as a present, just to show him how I felt about him, maybe he would twig that one? Of course not, he was too smart for that; he was above all of that. I could never match my brother when it came to academia, I went by the seat of my pants whereas he was mindful and the perfect student, so it was no contest, I hadn't a hope of gaining an advantage.

Except maybe when it came down to the brass tacks of reality, I was more street wise and had more local knowledge, especially when it came to pubs and the cool places to go. He definitely wasn't cool, and he stood out like a sore thumb with his invariably tactless comments to beautiful women and the like. He was like a polar bear in the Gobi Desert, people tried to avoid him as he was a patronising bollix. I would do my utmost in order to send him to the wrong pub when he would ask where I was going. None of my friends wanted him for too long in their company; he was a pain in the arse.

For years and years when all was calm and quiet, he used to come down for weekends and camp in the house for an interminably long time, he said that he had worked very hard and he felt he deserved the long breaks. Yet here was I stuck in the middle trying to get on with my working life and I had to avoid going home so many times over the years as I couldn't stand him being around the house, he was an awful messer, the house was treated like his personal trophy house, he could do as he pleased, it was the family home after all. He had absolutely no regard for my own peace and quiet or dignity, my own space. I left it go on for too long as I felt powerless to challenge him as it was after all the family home and it was up to me to toe the line and be put in my box constantly when I rebelled at this behaviour.

I felt so powerless and useless in the face of all these visits, I was like that little boy in the corner all over again, unable to make a call of my own, no independence in my own home. I had no escape, no peace of mind whilst he was around.

I'm in the psychiatric unit in Tralee, not wishing to see any visitors, but who walks in? He was the last person I wanted to see in my depressed state, I was never into small talk, I would have preferred to be in the team meetings rather than be in Tim's company, such was my abhorrence. However, you cannot escape from your own family, unless you move to Australia or somewhere remote, like Kalgoorlie, then it is fine to write from a distance, no hassle, just tell it as it is.

"Any which way you can", was my motto, but nobody else concurred. I was hopeless at mathematics, yet when it came to physics and very complicated equations, I found the answers in my own unique way.

Twenty years later, it was the same, when I devoured mathematical equations to calculate the ideal compression height in engine building, learnt equivalence ratios and gas flow ratios that controlled the fuel to air ratio inducted into a combustion chamber. But if you asked me to do a simple calculation, I couldn't do it. I ordered numerous books on the building of turbocharged engines long before they became the norm in production. These books came from the US, where pioneer developers were way ahead of their European compatriots long before it came to digital computerisation of management systems. After all these years, NASCAR racing in the US is only now changing over to fuel injection, but that was primarily to reduce costly electronic controls for the teams involved. Maybe it was a trust issue?

I am at home on a Friday evening, just beginning to relax when I hear someone at the front door. It was of course Tim, who decided to invite himself down for the weekend without my knowledge, thereby sending any plans I may have had for the weekend into a spin, I was back in meltdown, unable to come and go as I pleased. I would avoid going back to the house as I couldn't stand him being around for too long. But the weekend quickly became a week, and I had no inclination as to when he intended to return to Dublin. I used to drive into the estate and if I saw his car outside the door, I would turn around and go anywhere but home. It was so bad at one stage that I considered dumping all of his belongings outside on the driveway in the pouring rain just to get rid of him. It took a flaming row for me to get my message across and of course I had lost it according to all and sundry, yet nobody else in the family would put him up in their homes, I was goosed.

And so the battle still goes on, and my only hope is that when my poor mum has passed away, will I have any peace in my life, any space to call my own, maybe even invite someone in to share it with me if that should happen, Enchala.

Meanwhile back at the ranch, all is quiet, until the next unscheduled visit, where all peace and calm is blown to the wind and I'm left feeling like a headless chicken. Being told constantly "this is your making, this is your life now, you made it that way for yourself", and I'm back in the melting pot once again. How am I supposed to move on with my life? I don't need constant reminders about where I am now, why I'm there, and how it came to be. I feel like I'm out in the desert living in that nice little shelter out of the melting sun when suddenly all these people appear out of the sandstorm, looking to kip down for interminable lengths of time. Jesus help me!

I felt like a prisoner on probation, being constantly monitored and reminded by all and sundry that "You have a condition"; sure everyone has some condition or other, that's the way life is, take it or leave it. Well, I had been on death row for some time, but I survived the gas chamber and the spontaneous combustion. Some poor souls can't take it and suffer the ultimate punishment, yet they are generally lambasted afterwards by ordinary folk who have no idea what they have gone through. They don't see any options; maybe they don't have the means to get through the quagmire, which is akin to running through a minefield for most people. Why be judged by humanity and the system? They have to face their purgatory all alone in the melting heat of the moment.

What price does one have to pay for peace of mind? Where does the guilt stop? I have done more penance than most people, suffered horrendous emotional pain along the way. Why can't I move on from all of this and get back into the real world? All I really want is a little dignity, not having to beg for meagre crumbs along the way, not to be looked upon with suspicion and coldness, not to be admonished for being myself.

I just wanted a simple life, have enough to eat, a warm bed, mess with my bikes in the shed, work on my car, do a little bit of photography, dip into art, walk the mountains, cycle to my hearts content, and just enjoy the process. It's not too much to ask really. But I am starting to enjoy all of those activities again, though not at the frenetic pace of old. I had to learn how to breathe again, how to walk before running, how to manage anxiety, how to be positive and enjoy what life has to offer.

I kept being reminded about how lucky I was to be living in Killarney, right in the middle of the National park, with a stunning backdrop of mountains and lakes. But when you are depressed you cannot see beauty, anywhere. Killarney is the perfect outdoor antidote for anyone, especially so in the summer, that is if you get a summer. As my meltdown happened in Killarney, it was the last place I wanted to be seen in that condition. I was ashamed to be seen walking around aimlessly, my self respect diminished, my soul bared to all and sundry, it was humiliating. I would pass O Shea's funeral home and wonder to myself whether I'd be better off in there, it would be all over, no more torment.

Now, I have to get back into the real world. It's not easy trying to fit in, especially so when my meltdown was so obvious to all and sundry. I had lost faith in humanity, the kindness of people, the beauty of this wonderful place we live in. I had loved and lost, but there is always hope in this world. Technology has made communication so easy, yet it is very difficult to meet anyone to talk sensibly and honestly about their lives, their problems, it's like they just want to go with the tide, can't be bothered to chat about serious issues, with their mobiles sitting on the table in front of them as if they were expecting a call from Barrack Obama at any second, to change the world.

Karen used to talk about finding her "centre" so many times. I really had no idea what she meant at the time, but now, I know exactly what she meant. It took so many years, but at least I learnt the lesson. Whilst others run around like headless chickens, not knowing for one minute where their lives are going, I am right here, finding my own "centre", happy in the knowledge that I will no longer be influenced by the running pack of wolves, trying to fit in with other peoples perceptions of my life. Every day brings new challenges, new thinking, and new adventures

"How's the crack" is a regular saying used in social circles. Now there's a question that poses numerous questions and speculative answers. Well now, the crack today was very poor, as I was incarcerated by mental health services into solitary confinement, try and answer that one? Scurrying comes to mind, it's as if a guided missile was heading our way, all present in our company can't get away fast enough, are stunned by the thought and cannot begin to even think of an answer. They squirm away from the issue, shocked by this sudden bolt from the blue, and disappear in a flash. Try to bring up any mental health issues and they are lost, avoidance being the primary tactic.

In hindsight, I was always considered a little bit mad, but in a nice and funny kind of way. As I wore my heart on my sleeve, I was a moving target, what with my emotional sensitivity, my steely drive, my ferociously competitive spirit. I wanted to be the best, in whatever discipline it was, but it didn't transfer over into my academic abilities. I didn't care what anyone thought about me, I just went by the seat of my pants, whilst the reaction to me was baffled looks on people's faces, but I gave them plenty of laughs along the way.

The anger and rage within myself and the world at large is quickly abating, and I am more measured and appreciative of the difficulties some people find themselves in, that overwhelming anxiety that causes so much misery both to themselves and their families.

The real world has no place for people like this, with its unquenchable desire to wring more and more productivity out of people in the workplace, in their quest to make robots out of ordinary human beings in their lust for profits, bending over backward to please shareholders and bondholders to the detriment of the person.

It still hurts me when jobs are like gold dust in this lovely country of ours, where you are just a PPS number on Social Services, an outcast, frowned upon and disabled by society at large, and being classed as a scrounger. It hurt me deeply to have to seek dole money or whatever I was entitled to, it was so fucken degrading. I now understand what it is like when you wake up one morning to discover the carpet has been pulled from underneath you, with no safety net in place. Unfortunately, that is the case for many people, and most don't have the means to deal with it. Anxiety levels get so high that people cannot cope with life anymore, taking drastic measures to end the torment.

I wish there was a happy ending, but realistically, life can be numb and hostile to a large degree. It is incredibly lonesome living in this cocoon, having no soul mate, no real special one to share your thoughts with. The only real conversations happen to be with professionals working in the mental health arena.

Little did I know it at the time, but the only meaningful conversations I had for years were those I had with my Aunty Nora on her death bed. We seemed to be singing from the same hymn sheet. She understood more than anyone, my situation at home and my inability to cope with my ailing Mum, due to the meltdown I was suffering. She had unbelievable insight and was the most forward thinking woman I have ever met, despite her own failing health. She had the sharpest mind ever; right up until her organs began to fail.

I loved visiting Sr Nora in the Presentation Convent in Tralee. That building was so quiet and contemplative with all the nuns going about their daily prayer routine with dignity and calm. They were always so welcoming to me and poor Sr Nora would insist that I got a mug of milky coffee every time I visited, it had to be piping hot and frothy, or else she would urge me to get a fresh one. I envied them their peace and contentment, their endearment with a life of quiet and retreat form the every day world. For a brief moment, I felt happy in that atmosphere: no character assassination, no constant demands on me, and no unwelcome intrusions into my life, no bullshit.

Killarney never had any sense of community, It was every man for himself and especially so if you were in business. You couldn't keep suppliers happy as they kept trying to pressure you into buying more and more stuff even if it wasn't needed. There was no one to offer you a word of encouragement along the way, but there were plenty of people waiting to see you fall off your tiny perch. Begrudgery was very high in the scheme of things, just in case you might get ahead of yourself. Everything was judged by your ability to make money, any which way you could. It was incredibly snobbish in certain quarters, as attested to by my Aunty Nora in her early years in the convent, where she experienced favouritism and discrimination, mainly involving class distinction, totally distinct from any kind of race or sectarian bias.

Despite its terrible beauty, Killarney had its nay sayers by the truck load, high society revellers in abundance who seemed to think the poor working classes had no entitlements to play sport like golf and other elite sports, just because they didn't have the means available to indulge themselves in this manner, but neither did they have the inclination to mix it with the wafflers of high society. There were always society cliques operating in Killarney, where they turned their noses up at anyone trying to invade their clique, it was as if you needed a stamp of approval before they could chat with you. If you were a high flier or a man of means, then they would swarm over you hoping to get a bite of the cherry, but god help you if you fell on hard times, they vanished like a ghost, leaving you at the mercy of your PPS number.

I must forget all that crap and move on from the small minded thinking that is endemic in a small town like Killarney; thank god for the tourists come summer, at least you could have a decent conversation with them, no matter where they came from. You could extrapolate to your hearts content and then laugh about it afterwards, there was no hidden agenda.

I still think about that little tin shed out in the West Australian outback of Kalgoorlie, I think I was on to a good thing there, there is always hope! On the other hand, I'm stuck here on my own, until the next family member visits and takes over the reigns of control of the house for an unforeseen time and at their own pleasure, disregarding any preferences I may have in my own destiny, thrown to the wolves yet again. The prognosis is not good; it never can be in this kind of situation. How am I supposed to develop as a human being? Its gone way beyond that realm now, I am only surviving, playing a reluctant host to the frequent callers who appear all too often out of the blue.

I have made my peace with God, so everything else should be water off a ducks back for me. I am able to walk tall on my own again, not to worry about what people think of me. I am my own man again, thank god; I don't care what anybody thinks about me. I need not make excuses any more, I will just plough my own lonesome furrow in the vain hope that someone may like to follow me on occasions along the way, and if they don't, so what, I will survive, I can cope now with anything thrown at me, I am armed with the means to battle on regardless, come hell or high-water. I was always a strong swimmer!

THE END

Michael + Mary Fuller

Declan Fuller
+
David.

064 66 32955